INVESTIGATING

A Do-It-Yoursel

Written by Richard Whittell

Layout and design by Simon Saunders

First published 2014 by the Corporate Watch Cooperative Ltd
c/o Freedom Press
Angel Alley
84b Whitechapel High Street
London, E1 7QX
02074260005
contact@corporatewatch.org
www.corporatewatch.org

Picture credits, front page: Shutterstock

British Library Cataloguing in Publication Data
A catalogue record for this book is available from the British Library

ISBN 978-1-907738-15-9

Corporate Watch

CONTENTS

QUICK LINKS

INTRODUCTION

This handbook is designed to help you find out what you need to understand and challenge companies that are messing you or other people around. The more you know about a company, the more effective your challenge can be, and if you know where to look, you may be surprised at how much you can find.

Part 1 gives research tips and introduces various ways to find information about a company, including guides to using the web, and talking to employees, the company itself and people affected by its actions.

Part 2 introduces key legal and financial concepts for understanding companies. It explains the basics of company law, describes different types of companies, and gives introductions to corporate structures and finances. It ends with a longer section on how to read and understand accounts.

Part 3 shows you where to look to find specific information about a company. It describes and explains how to find sources from companies themselves, the business information industry, government, the media and campaigns. It concludes with an introductory guide to making Freedom of Information requests to public bodies.

> **NOTE**: Because websites change, the full addresses of the sites or pages referenced in the handbook aren't written out in full. However, a web search for the names as written will take you to the appropriate site, so if you enter it into your search engine you should find it.

The focus throughout is on UK companies but most of the information is relevant to companies wherever they are based.

Good luck! Use the contents, quick links, index and signposts within the text to find the bits that are useful to you, and thumb through directly to them. If anything isn't clear, or if you think something has been missed, please contact Corporate Watch at the details above.

ACKNOWLEDGEMENTS

The handbook has greatly benefited from the content, edits and expertise provided by Rebecca Fisher, Tom Anderson, Christina Laskaridis, Beth Lawrence, Patrick Morello, Michael Rogers, Mr EBs and everyone who worked on Corporate Watch's 2002 How to Research Corporations guide.

Thanks also to Luke Christie, Hanneke Hart, Jane Laporte, George Lavender, Taimour Lay, Phil Miller, Meesha Nehru, Ross Raisin, Andrew Robertson, Kezia Rolfe, Clare Sambrook, Jan Savage, Ellie Schling, Nick Sommerlad, John Whittell, Shiar Youssef and Yussi for their comments and advice, and to the Joseph Rowntree Reform Trust for their support.

PART 1
INVESTIGATING

TOP TIPS

There's no single, 'right' way to investigate a company, so don't feel like you have to be an expert to do it well. In general, the more you persist and persevere, the more you'll find. Below are some basic pointers to help you get started.

KNOW WHAT YOU WANT

There's a huge amount of information that you could find out about a company but not all of it will be useful. Chances are you'll only have a limited amount of time, so make sure you're sticking to the stuff you need by targeting your research as much as possible.

Are you interested in a company's operations or history? Its finances? What it's doing in other parts of the world? Who owns it? What its legal responsibilities are? Who else is having problems with it? How it justifies its operations? Or something else?

And what are you planning to do with the information you find? Do you need to find information to support claims or demands you are making, or to negotiate with one of the company's representatives? Are you looking to make a short leaflet to hand round your local area, a more comprehensive report on the company, or are you trying to put together a legal case against it?

What you are looking for will determine who you speak to, and which part of the company and which sources you look at.

Keep in mind your end goal and make sure you're looking for something because it's what you need, not just because it's interesting. Don't waste time digging up facts that you know you're not going to use.

Use the quick links page at the front of the handbook to help you find what you need.

STRUCTURE YOUR RESEARCH

It's impossible to perfectly plan everything in advance, but making a plan and structuring your research at the beginning will save you time in the long run, even if it is a bit boring to do first up.

After you've worked out what you want to know, make a list of all the possible sources you could go to. Prioritise those you think are most likely to lead to the most useful information and try to plan how long you're going to spend on each of them.

As a general rule of thumb, for example, it'll probably make sense to get as far as you can with your research before letting the company know that you're looking into it. That way, you'll be well-prepared for its spin and you can choose the most effective questions to get the most revealing answers.

FIND OUT WHAT ELSE HAS BEEN DONE

Especially if you're looking at a big company, the information you're looking for may have been found already. Put aside some time at the beginning of your investigation to find out what has already been done. You may save yourself a lot of time.

RECORD YOUR REFERENCES

This is another boring one but it's important.

If you log things like names, phone numbers, details of where and when you found a piece of information and when you accessed a website, you can save yourself time in the long run. If later in your investigations you come to doubt some of your information, you can easily go back and check your sources if you have a clear record. And being able to go back to them may give you new leads.

Photograph or video evidence where necessary and keep photocopies of all useful paper sources. Take printouts of web pages, or save them onto your hard drive.

FOLLOW SOURCES AND LEADS

Always keep an eye out for potential sources of information. Ask anyone you talk to if they know anyone else you should try.

Where possible, look at the sources used in an article or report yourself and see if they contain any extra information. If it's not clear, call up whoever wrote the article or did the research and ask them where they got their information from.

Follow the links from useful websites and always look through bibliographies and reference lists in publications.

Don't get side-tracked, but stay on the lookout for – and be keen to investigate – possible new sources of information.

BE AWARE OF THE BIASES AND LIMITATIONS OF SOURCES

Can you trust your source? Be sceptical. Be alert to the bias of the article, website or person giving you information.

A company and its senior staff are bound to stress the positive.

Media, business information sources, trade unions, people affected by the company, campaigns and 'official' government sources may all have their biases too.

Always cross-check information: even the most decent and honourable people can get their facts wrong.

THE WEB

If you have access to a computer and an internet connection, you'll no doubt be using the web to find lots of the information you want about a company. It can be a very useful and convenient way to research, giving you access to an ever-expanding treasure trove of information, but it can also lead to hours of time wasted as you get further away from what you went on the web for in the first place.

Get off the web when you've found what you want and look for leads and sources but don't aimlessly follow links. It's always tempting to see how Robbie Williams and Gary Barlow are getting on, but clicking on that link is not going to help you find out how much the directors of the major oil companies are making.

See section 1.6 for important security issues to bear in mind while searching the web.

SEARCH ENGINES

Software systems that 'crawl' the web for information that they then store in a database are known as search engines. They index the information they find, so the most relevant results for a particular search can be retrieved as quickly as possible – by key word, date, language and so on.

Helping people search the web has become extremely profitable and the owners of the best-known search engines – Google being the most obvious – are among the biggest companies in the world. The most noticeable sign of this commercialisation is the ever-increasing number of adverts that litter search results pages. Some of these look a lot like 'genuine' links. so be careful what you're clicking on.

Type a word into a search engine and it can yield hundreds of thousands of pages so it's good to narrow it down as much as possible.

Search engines are getting better at working out what you're looking for but it's still useful to know how to get best results from your searches as quickly as possible.

The most important advice is the most obvious: **choose your words well**.

But you can save time by telling your search engine to search in a particular way, by typing search instructions together with the words you are searching for.

Some of the more useful search instructions include:

QUOTATION MARKS

Putting two or more words in "quotation marks" is a way of telling the search engine to look for them together, in the order you've typed them, and not for all the times they occur separately.

If you're looking for a specific report, for example, put the title in quotation marks. Searching for "Investigating Companies: A Do-It-Yourself Handbook" would bring up this guide.

You can use quotation marks to search for a quote in order to find its source.

SITE:

This specifies the type of organisation whose website you want to search. Searching for *corporate lobbying site:org.uk* for example, will give results on corporate lobbying from campaign groups and other organisations whose websites have the .org.uk domain name.

site:gov.uk and site:ac.uk will do the same for UK government and educational institutions.

This can be very useful to get a non-corporate view of the world, as companies and corporate media sites spend lots of money on 'search engine optimisation' – i.e. getting their site higher up in search results – so when you look for a common term, the most popular results will often be from corporate sites.

You can use this to search particular websites. Searching for *corporate lobbying site:www.bbc.co.uk* for example, gives you articles on the issue just from the BBC. Searching for *corporate lobbying site:www.mining-journal.com* would give you articles from the mining industry's trade journal.

You can search websites from a particular country by using the country domain.

site:se for example, only gives you pages from Sweden.

MINUS SIGN

This excludes words from a search. *Prince –William* will give you results about the purple musician and the brand of tennis balls, but not the royal heir.

INURL:

This searches for particular words in a URL (web address). **Intitle:** does the same within the title of a webpage.

:DOC, :PPT, :PDF

Useful if you're looking for something you know is in a particular type of file, such as a word document, powerpoint presentation or a pdf.

RELATED:

This helps you find similar websites, although search engines can make odd choices. Type in *related:www.corporatewatch.org* into Google and you'll get the U.S. Chamber of Commerce (motto: "Standing Up for American Enterprise").

ADVANCED SEARCH

Some search engines allow you to specify the date a page or article was published (for example, within the last week, month, year). You can also specify the language you want the results to be in and which country they are from, among other things. Many search engines contain **specialised databases** that can give you a different set of results from their usual search engines. Most now have 'News' and 'Images' as options, and Google has patent and academic article searches, for example. These can narrow your results substantially.

SAVING WEB PAGES

The web is not static: information can move about, or even vanish completely. Companies who know they are being watched may deliberately take down material.

Use the 'save page as' function in your browser to save a copy of a webpage onto your hard drive, or print it off or take a screenshot (usually done by pressing the Prt Sc button on your keyboard). That way you ensure you have a record of it and you can access it at a later date.

ARCHIVE SEARCHES

Material on the web is always changing. Internet archive sites such as the Wayback Machine, which has been crawling the internet for almost twenty years and storing old versions of websites, can help you find previous versions of pages that have since been changed. Type the name of the website or page you're interested in into the Wayback site's search box and you'll be able to find previous versions from a range of dates.

If the website you're looking for has been completely deleted, you can search Google's cache (store) of pages

CASE STUDY: Brighton-based arms company EDO MBM removed several pages from its website relating to the manufacture of a controversial bomb rack and arming unit shortly before its Managing Director was due to give evidence in court at the trial of campaigners arrested for a protest against the company.

However, by using the Way Back Machine web archive, campaigners were able to recover the pages, making the director's questioning even more uncomfortable than he had anticipated.

it has examined in the past to find the last active version (search "how to use google cache" for instructions on how to do this as it may depend on the browser you're using).

LIBRARIES

Even though so much is now online, you can still find lots of information in public libraries that you wouldn't find through searching the web. Books about a company or its industry, or the directories and journals listed in Part 3 of this handbook may be free to read in a library but paywalled or inaccessible online. You can also access online databases that are usually paywalled from the computers in some libraries. The business section of a borough's central library is likely to be an especially useful resource.

Just like on the web, browsing can result in some interesting discoveries, but beware of getting side-tracked. Ask library assistants which book is best for your purposes or search the catalogue - using subject keywords, author or publisher.

Libraries are being hit hard by the current government's cuts to public spending, with 200 branches closing in 2012 and others having to limit their book-buying. If your local library doesn't have what you need, ask the librarian if they can get a copy through the interlibrary loan service. Failing that, try:

COPYRIGHT LIBRARIES

There are five in the UK - the British Library, the national libraries of Scotland and Wales, and those of Oxford and Cambridge universities. By law they are entitled to receive a copy of every publication published in the UK. The library of Trinity College, Dublin is also covered by this legislation.

The most comprehensive is the British Library in London, where the law stipulates that a copy of every publication must be sent. To use copyright libraries, you will need to register by filling in a form and explaining that they have resources you can't get elsewhere. Most keep their collections in stack storage so you may save time by ordering the publications you want in advance of your visit.

SPECIALIST AND BUSINESS LIBRARIES

There are several around the UK, stocking a wide range of trade journals, business directories and other useful sources. Ask at your local library for details of the nearest.

Many government departments or industry bodies, such as trade associations and professional institutions, have libraries of their own. These can be a great source of information - assuming you can persuade them to let you in. Some will charge.

UNIVERSITY LIBRARIES

They usually have good reference sources, including trade journals and directories. Universities vary in how willing they are to give access to non-students however.

OUT AND ABOUT

You can access lots of the sources in this handbook from a computer or in print, but there's often no substitute for getting away from the desk, talking to people and seeing what you can find. Go down to the company's offices or workplace, see what things look like, and if the company is complying with regulations and standards. You may also find out who is supplying the company with goods and services, or who their business partners are. Take a camera to photograph or video what you find. But often the most valuable information will come from people with personal experience of the company.

TALK TO PEOPLE AFFECTED BY THE COMPANY

If you want to know the impact of a company's operations, talk to people affected by them. If you have suffered from the company's activities yourself, it's still worth talking to other people to get different experiences and perspectives – and a bigger body of evidence.

Go down to the areas where the company is working and ask people about it. Knock on doors or try local pubs or cafes.

Contact existing campaigns and community groups working on the issue (see section 3.2 for more on this). Take a leaflet or card with your contact details on that people can take if they don't want to talk to you in public.

Back at the computer, see if there are any online forums that you can get in touch with people through, such as a Facebook group, or if they have LinkedIn or Twitter profiles. You could tweet out general requests to ask people who have information on a particular subject to get in touch with you.

Remember, gaining people's trust can take time, and people are often more

CASE STUDY: Working against workfare

Workfare – forcing unemployed people to work without pay for companies and other organisations – was introduced in the UK by New Labour. Anti-poverty and claimants' groups – some of whose members had been forced to do unpaid placements – started to piece together a list of which companies were benefiting from it by talking to people about it as they were leafleting their local jobcentres.

As the scale of the scheme became clear and the coalition expanded it further – with huge companies like Tesco, Asda, Argos and Primark benefiting from thousands of hours of free labour – the groups started the Boycott Workfare campaign that has since shamed many companies, plus charities and other organisations, into pulling out of the scheme.

likely to talk to you if they can see that

you're not there just to report on what's going on, but to help them change it. Don't assume people will be happy with you quoting them or taking photos – always ask permission. **Always respect requests for anonymity** and make sure you have people's permission to use their name publicly.

Where relevant, ask people if they can provide you with as much evidence to back up what they are saying as possible, not necessarily because you doubt them, but because the more evidence you have, the more effective you can be.

TALK TO DISGRUNTLED WORKERS

The people who work for the company can tell you more about it than most, and contact with staff members who are willing to help you can lead you to discoveries you wouldn't otherwise be able to make.

A useful first step may be to get in touch with their trade union. Try to talk to workers as well as the union officers – and the local branch as well as national head office – as their views and opinions can sometimes differ.

If the company works with the government or a public sector body, talk to staff there. They may be particularly willing to talk if the service they work for is slated for privatisation, or if they're unhappy with the deal provided by the company.

Civil servants, and staff of executive agencies, regulators or local councils can give you lots of good information if you can persuade them to talk to you.

If you come into contact with a staff member who wants to 'blow the whistle', and release sensitive information about

the company they're working for, encourage them but appreciate that this could have serious consequences on their lives, and be supportive and respectful of their choices.

Minimise risk by not communicating with them through their company email account and take other precautions as necessary (see the guides mentioned on pages 16 and 17). Only publish information they give you with their consent, and ensure that you are taking as much care as necessary to protect their interests.

TALK TO RIVAL COMPANIES

Your enemy's enemy isn't exactly your friend, but if you can get talking to someone from a rival company, they may give you some good information or maybe just some interesting gossip on their competitors. Just make sure that you're not a pawn in a game they're playing.

GOING UNDERCOVER

If you have the time and inclination, you could try to get a job with the company you're looking into.

Going undercover in this way can lead you to all sorts of valuable information and discoveries, but there are various concerns to bear in mind, especially if you want to publish the information you find. Among others, you risk being charged with fraud for false representation – as you were paid for a job you got on the basis of a false CV – and the contract you sign will more than likely contain a confidentiality clause, opening yourself up to a civil claim by the company.

TALKING TO THE COMPANY

Putting questions or accusations to the company you're looking at can lead to new information and it can be a good way of testing what you've found. The company may confirm your findings, or they may say you've got the wrong end of the stick and produce solid evidence to show why. If so, it's better to know this before you go public.

To get a **formal response from the company as a whole,** for example to accusations that you are making against it, you're probably best off calling the main contact number or, if they have one, the press office or media centre. If they think it's worth their while to engage with you they will, even if you're not from the media. If it's a small company, you could also go straight to a director.

If you're looking for information, rather than a formal response, it may be better to **talk to the individual member of staff** responsible for the part of the company's work that you're interested in. Give them a call directly if you have their number, ask to be transferred through the main switchboard, send them an email or go down to their workplace. See page 67 and section 3.5 for more on finding details of directors and senior members of staff.

You could also go to **industry events**, such as expos, conferences, exhibitions and corporate award ceremonies. These events are designed to be hobnobbing opportunities for corporate executives as well as a chance for corporations to network and market themselves, and to make deals. You may find government officials there too. Companies sometimes hand out information at these events that is not available in the public domain. Arms companies, for example, have been known to give out details of illegal weaponry at arms fairs. You can often gain access to these events quite easily – for some it's as simple as going on the organiser's website and registering. For more controversial exhibitions you might need a cover story. See page 79 for a list of corporate events organisers.

If you're **part of a campaign**, use the access to senior staff you sometimes get as a result of a protest, action or other event to ask them questions, or ask them to confirm or deny accusations.

Here are a few tips for getting useful information from interviews or interactions with people from the company you're looking into:

PREPARE BEFORE

Check your facts and brush up on your background knowledge. Choose your questions in advance and make them as precise and understandable as possible so you don't waste time with genuine misunderstandings. It might be helpful to practice with somebody.

Think about the tone you want to take in advance. In general, making eye contact, not interrupting, keeping your emotions in check and being polite but firm are good default modes, but there may be times when more adversarial or friendly approaches may work better. Try to think about the issue from the company's point of view to anticipate possible responses. They may shut up shop and get suspicious if you ask about something particularly sensitive, so leave those questions till last and get the less controversial ones in first.

KNOW WHO YOU ARE

You may decide that you'll get more information if you use an assumed identity. This will depend on what you're asking for. If you want a company to confirm or deny accusations you are making, it may make more sense to say who you really are: if they think you will publicise your findings, they may want to correct anything you've got wrong. If you start a dialogue like this, remember that you're there to get information about the company, not give it about you. But if you're looking to pry out information they wouldn't usually give, using an alias may work better. Make sure you've thought it through and are prepared for questions they may ask about you.

Remember that if you're making contact over email they'll probably search the name you give on the web. They're unlikely to give out sensitive information if they doubt your cover story.

DOCUMENT YOUR INTERVIEW

Note the time, place, who you spoke to and their position, any alias you used, major points and important quotes. Do this during or immediately after your interviews – most of us forget details surprisingly quickly. Record it if possible so you can confirm and verify any good quotes you get.

You're under no legal obligation to tell the interviewee you're recording them on a video camera or dictaphone if you're not going to share it with others. If you do publish or distribute it, you'd need to show that your actions were in the public interest if your interviewee chose to sue. If somebody talks to you 'off the record', they don't expect you to publish what they say. If you do, they're unlikely to talk to you again.

LOOK THROUGH THE JARGON

A response, especially a written one, from a company may well be corporate fluff that doesn't really answer your questions. If you want to check if you are correct about something, reiterate or rephrase your question or accusation and ask the company to confirm or deny specific points.

If they just deny something without providing supporting evidence – or they deny a slightly different question to the one you asked, then keep asking until you get a proper answer. If nothing is forthcoming, that may be an answer in itself. Don't let them schmooze you.

KNOW WHEN TO STOP

If the person you're talking to offers to send you a useful document, consider ending the interview there. Wait until you've actually received what they send, then contact them again with more questions if you have them. If you're trying to pry information out of a wary staff member, you may be better not asking for anything too sensitive the first time you talk, unless you think that will be the only chance you are going to get.

STAYING SAFE

Companies sometimes go to great lengths to watch the people watching them. Some have hired spies to infiltrate groups digging into them and police have placed undercover officers into anti-corporate campaigns. Be especially careful if you're looking into an issue that's seen as controversial, or is of interest to the police. In some cases, people investigating companies profiting from Israeli settlements in Palestine have been detained under terrorism legislation when crossing UK borders, while people looking into arms companies have had their houses searched and computers confiscated. Keep copies of your findings in different places if you're worried. Have a look at the **Activist Security Handbook**, the **Journalist Security Guide,** both available online, and the **Green & Black Cross** website for more information on security and your rights.

WEB SEARCH SECURITY

More and more evidence is emerging that our internet usage is not as private as we might like. Companies known as data brokers profit from tracking people's search and browsing histories, building profiles of internet users, and selling them to advertisers and other clients.

This is big business – the data brokerage industry involves an estimated 4,000 companies, with combined annual revenue of more than $150 billion. States track people's internet usage too: EU law, for example, requires internet service providers to record information about their customers' internet usage and make that information available to government agencies. Recent revelations about the US government's National Security Agency have highlighted the extent to which it collects information on internet users around the world.

Whenever you visit a web page your visit may be recorded by your internet service provider, the website itself, and other sites that provide parts of the page, such as advertisements and social media buttons.

Any of those entities can track you by labelling your visits to different web pages as visits by the same person, in order to build a profile of your interests and activities. Some sites may ask for personal details such as your name, which can then be combined with your visits to other sites to build a more complete profile.

Search engines, social networking sites and email providers have especially detailed information about their visitors, and it is no coincidence that Google – which provides all of the above – is the largest data broker.

The easiest way for sites to track you is through your IP address – a number that uniquely identifies your connection to the internet. Another widespread method of tracking is to use cookies – small pieces of data stored on your computer by websites you visit. Cookies can also be stored by sites that provide parts of the pages you visit, such as advertisements or social media buttons. These are known as third-party cookies, and they are a powerful way to track visitors across multiple sites.

You can reduce your susceptibility to tracking by taking a few simple steps:

CONFIGURE YOUR WEB BROWSER

Set it to reject third-party cookies and delete all cookies, history and cache (where your browser temporarily stores pages you have visited) when the browser is closed. In addition, most popular browsers now have options for 'private browsing', which means they should not store your browsing information for that session (though we can't verify these claims). In Firefox, this is called 'private browsing'; in Chrome, it's called 'incognito'.

CHOOSE A SAFER SEARCH ENGINE

Some of the smaller ones have stricter privacy policies than Google, Bing and the other majors. Duckduckgo and ixquick say they do not store IP addresses or collect or share any personal information, though we cannot vouch for how accurate this is. If you use Google, the GoogleSharing add-on for Firefox claims to prevent it from tracking your searches.

LOG OUT OF EMAIL/SOCIAL MEDIA

Google and other commercial providers link your searches to your account if you're signed in, so it's worth signing out before doing sensitive searches. Likewise, signing out of social networks when you're not using them will reduce the chances of tracking cookies being linked to your social media accounts.

USE TOR OR A VPN

Tor is software that enables you to browse the web privately and anonymously by redirecting your internet connection through a network of volunteer-operated 'relay' computers around the world. This conceals your IP address from the sites you visit, and hides those sites from your internet service provider. The simplest and safest way to use Tor is to download the Tor Browser Bundle, a web browser based on Mozilla Firefox that is customised for use with Tor. You can download it for free from the torproject website.

Other projects use 'proxy servers' or 'virtual private networks' (VPNs) to securely route your traffic through their servers in order to anonymise your location and prevent others from spying on your internet traffic. Examples of the latter include Riseup's VPN. Commercial sites such as hidemyass claim to allow you to search the web anonymously, but they will hand over your identity if legally required to do so.

You may want to take further precautions to protect your emails and the data stored on your computer. Applications and techniques are always being developed to increase people's security, many of which are free to use. For more information on security see the following guides, all available online:

- ❑ Tech Tools for Activism
- ❑ Basic Internet Security
- ❑ Open Rights Group
- ❑ Security In-a-Box
- ❑ Surveillance Self-Defense

DEFAMATION

Companies have sued members of the public and campaigners for defamation, or for unfairly harming their reputation (libel is written or recorded defamation, as opposed to slander, which is spoken). Publishing or sharing a defamatory statement about an identifiable individual or company with a third party – for example through an email, leaflet, tweet or newspaper article – puts you at risk so it's worth being aware of the threat when you're looking for information that you intend to share.

The 2013 Defamation Act stipulates that for-profit companies have not suffered serious harm unless the statement has caused "serious financial loss", which they have to prove. At the time of writing the Act has only just been passed so it is not clear what will be deemed serious, though it will likely depend on the size of the company. For individuals, for example company directors, a statement is defamatory if its publication has caused – or is likely to cause – "serious harm" to their reputation.

Defamation law is very complicated and we're not going to attempt to give more than a few pointers here. Make sure you choose your words and phrases carefully and that you can back them all up with solid, reliable sources. The test is how they would be understood by a "reasonable reader" so try to imagine how somebody else who did not necessarily share your views or analysis would understand them. You are at risk if an incorrect inference can be drawn from what you write, even if you did not intend it.

You can argue that what you published was true but the onus will be on you to prove it. You can also argue that your statement was on a matter of public interest and that you 'reasonably believed' publishing it was in the public interest. You may have to show that you were not acting with 'malice' and that you did your best to act responsibly, for example by taking steps to verify your statement. Asking the company or individual for their side of the story may help with this.

You can argue 'honest opinion' – 'here's my opinion on a matter of public interest and it is not based on lies' – as long as what you write is clearly presented as comment or opinion and not fact. Satire can be a refuge when your facts are uncertain but you want to make your point. The less reliable your sources, the more you'll require corroboration from additional sources. Use of devices such as 'according to ...' and 'allegedly' may help but they are not automatic get-outs.

If you receive a letter threatening defamation action, don't panic. Read it carefully to see if there's anything to it before changing anything. Ask exactly what you are being accused of if you're not sure. If you realise you have made a mistake, retract the false claim as soon as possible. Be aware that the law says you have to show you did everything you could as soon as practically possible to correct the inaccurate information.

See the **Centre for Investigate Journalism**'s free guide to libel law, available on their website, or the book **McNae's Essential Libel Law for Journalists**, for more information.

PART 2
UNDERSTANDING
THE COMPANY

COMPANY LAW

In the UK, companies are formed and regulated under the Companies Act, the most recent version of which was passed in 2006. Companies are also governed by a host of laws, regulations and codes, in particular the Insolvency Act 1986 and, for publicly-quoted companies, the UK Corporate Governance Code. (see page 81 for legal cases and specific legislation and regulations). When people create, or, in the jargon, 'incorporate' a company, they set up a body with certain legal characteristics:

SEPARATE LEGAL ENTITY

When a company is incorporated, it takes on its own 'legal personality', distinct in the eyes of the law from its shareholders, directors and employees. This means companies have legal rights and duties, and can enter into legal relationships – they can sue or be sued, own property, enter into contracts, and claim rights to a fair trial, privacy and freedom of expression. Companies can be prosecuted for wrongdoing under criminal legislation in the UK but, as they cannot be jailed, the main punishment available is a fine.

SHARES AND SHAREHOLDERS

All profit-making companies have a certain number of shares (a 'share capital') that give their owners (the 'shareholders') the right to vote on a range of issues, including the direction of the company's business – usually on the principle of one share one vote – and the right to receive 'dividend' payments from the company's profits, and a share of its worth if it is wound up. The number of shares issued by a company is normally decided by a shareholder vote.

If shareholders, who are also called 'members', sell their shares, the rights and benefits from the shares are transferred to the new owners. See section 3.1 for how to find out who a company's shareholders are, and page 54 for dividends.

LIMITED LIABILITY AND THE 'CORPORATE VEIL'

The personal liability of shareholders in the majority of UK companies is limited to the value of their investment in the company. This means that if a company becomes insolvent, its shareholders lose what their shares cost, but are not personally liable for the company's debts. Lenders, suppliers or staff owed money and wages have a right to the company's cash and possessions ahead of the shareholders but they have no claim on the shareholders' personal wealth. This principle also means that the company, but not its shareholders, is responsible for criminal or civil claims brought against it. It has proven very difficult to 'pierce the corporate veil' that is provided by incorporation. Even if a company is convicted of, say, corporate manslaughter, its shareholders will not normally be held personally liable. However, in certain limited cases, directors or employees may be prosecuted if they are personally responsible for criminal behaviour while working for the company.

INCORPORATION: A VERY BRIEF HISTORY

Pre-1600: Concept of 'incorporation' develops to provide independent legal identity for non-commercial institutions, such as hospitals, monasteries and colleges, so they can exist independently of their founders.

1600: East India Company, a forerunner of the modern multinational, established by Royal Charter to pursue trade in the "East Indies" (South and East Asia).

1844: Joint Stock Companies Act allows companies to register themselves without a specific charter.

1855: Britain passes the Limited Liabilities Act – becoming the first country to limit the liability of the members of certain companies to the value of their shares.

1856: New Joint Stock Companies Act simplifies the administrative procedure allowing incorporation of limited liability companies and forms the basis of future UK company law.

2006: Most recent Companies Act, based on the principles of the 1856 act.

See Corporate Watch's Corporate Law and Structures report for a more detailed history

Note that some companies are set up to be **unlimited companies**. As the name suggests, the legal liability of their shareholders is not limited to the cost of their shares and they are personally liable for its debts in the event of insolvency.

Perhaps unsurprisingly, most companies in the UK are limited. There are certain financial, legal and administrative reasons why investors may set up an unlimited company. They may be confident there is a low risk of insolvency, or they may want to avoid the disclosure requirements for limited companies (unlimited companies do not have to publish annual accounts, for example).

CORPORATION OR COMPANY:
What's the difference between a corporation and a company? Most of the time, the terms can be used interchangeably – all companies are incorporated and therefore are technically corporations.

The word corporation tends to be used for big companies that operate in different countries, often further described as multinational or transnational corporations. 'Corporation' also includes other incorporated legal entities, such as town councils or the City of London corporation.

DIRECTORS

In general, the bigger the company, the more directors it will have.

☐ The Chief Executive Officer (CEO) is the director in overall charge of the management of the company. Also known as the Managing Director or Chief Executive.

☐ The Chief Operating Officer (COO) is responsible for the day-to-day running of the company's work and the Chief Financial Officer (CFO) is in charge of financial planning and reporting.

☐ Non-executive directors are not responsible for the day-to-day running of the company but their role is typically to oversee its overall operations and governance. They sit on the company's board of directors and in large companies are often senior corporate or political figures who add to the company's reputation and connections.

☐ The chairman or chairwoman of the board may be an executive or non-executive director, and may hold some other office with the company.

In practice, the more diversified the ownership of a company, the more power the directors may have. Companies that publicly-list their shares may have hundreds or thousands of shareholders and few with enough shares to influence the direction of the business on their own, which may give the directors more influence than if they had to answer to only one or two shareholders.

This can give directors the opportunity to prioritise their own, or their employees', interests over those of the shareholders (by proposing inflated salaries or bonuses, for example).

DIRECTORS' DUTIES

Shareholders often delegate the day-to-day management of the company to directors (many people, of course, both own and run companies and, in this case, the shareholders may also be directors). In the UK, employees are not allowed to vote on company resolutions or the hiring and firing of directors, as they are in some other countries.

Unlike shareholders, directors are not protected by the corporate veil. They can be fined for breaches of certain duties under relevant legislation, or disqualified from holding directorships for a period. In certain limited cases, they may also be charged with criminal offences in relation to the operation of a company.

Directors must act within the powers

granted by the company's Articles of Association and any Memorandum of Association, and are bound by certain legal responsibilities – known as '**fiduciary duties**'. Section 172 of the UK Companies Act sets out that a director "must act in the way he considers, in good faith, would be most likely to promote the success of the company for the benefit of its members as a whole".

Although the act says a director must "have regard" to a number of other matters, including the interests of the company's employees and the impact of its operations on the community and the environment, the key measurement of "success" is most-often seen as the profitability of the company.

The Directors' Duties briefing by the Taylor Wessing law firm, free to read online, gives further details. See page 67 for how to find out who the directors of a company are.

TAX

In the UK, companies pay corporation tax on their profits. Shareholders may then have to pay tax on any dividends they receive and employees have to pay personal income tax and national insurance on their wages. VAT is added on to the price of many products and services.

Tax regulations are notoriously complicated and regularly change, so check the HMRC website for up-to-date rules and rates.

Some companies try to pay as little tax as possible, often by shifting their profits to countries with low tax rates. See section 2.6 for how to find out how much tax a company is paying.

WINDING UP/LIQUIDATION

When companies stop doing business they go into liquidation, their assets and property are distributed and they cease to exist. The most common reason for the winding up of a company is insolvency through lack of cash, meaning it cannot pay its debts on time.

In this case, creditors – the people the company owes money to – may commence insolvency proceedings against it, or the directors may choose to instigate the winding up process themselves.

There are various insolvency procedures available and creditors may prefer to avoid liquidation if they can achieve a better outcome from a company's rescue. These include a company voluntary arrangement or administration. These types of procedures may give the company more time to pay off its debts, or may enable some of them to be reduced or extinguished.

If liquidation becomes inevitable, an appointed 'liquidator' will adjudicate creditors claims and collect and distribute the company's possessions accordingly. There are various claims that can be brought against directors if there is evidence of wrongdoing on their part.

If the company has not run into trouble but has chosen to stop doing business voluntarily (after a resolution has been passed by shareholders), its assets are redistributed to creditors, and whatever is left goes to the shareholders.

Directors then file for its dissolution, after which it is struck off the register of companies at Companies House.

TYPES OF COMPANY

The majority of limited companies in the UK are **private companies limited by shares** - indicated by the abbreviation 'Ltd'.

A **public limited company** - or **plc** - has the legal characteristics described in section 2.1, but its shares can be sold to the general public through stock exchanges such as the London Stock Exchange.

This increases the amount of investment it can attract (see section 2.5) but plcs are subject to more regulations, and have to disclose more information than private limited companies (see section 3.1).

Most big, multinational companies are plcs. Note that the 'public' in their name doesn't mean they're owned by the government or the state.

Plcs are also called publicly-traded, listed or quoted companies. Note that a company must have the legal form of a plc if it wants to have its shares listed on an exchange but not every plc chooses to list its shares.

Some companies do not have shares but are limited by guarantee. Private **companies limited by guarantee** are usually set up to be not-for-profit and do not have shareholders but 'members'. They also have a separate legal personality and their members are protected by limited liability, but instead of liability being limited to the value of the shares, they guarantee to pay a - usually very small - nominal amount. They also use the Ltd abbreviation. Unless stated otherwise, 'company' or 'companies' in this guide refers to profit-making limited companies.

> **ABBREVIATIONS**: Countries use different abbreviations to signify types of company. Alternatives for Ltd include:
>
> SARL (French-speaking countries)
> GMBH (Germany)
> Pty (Australia and South Africa)
> Inc (US)
> BV (Netherlands)

> **TRADING NAMES**: Companies may not be widely known by the official name they register at Companies House, and the 'trading name' they use for their day-to-day business may be different. Companies will usually at least drop the 'Ltd' or the 'plc'. Vodafone Group plc, for example, just goes by Vodafone.

Other types of business or trading organisation in the UK include:

SELF-EMPLOYED/SOLE TRADER

Individuals running a business in a personal capacity, rather than incorporating a company and running it through that.

PARTNERSHIP

In a partnership, two or more people run a business in common and all the partners share responsibility for it. Profits and losses can be shared between the partners and each partner pays tax on their share of the profits.

In England, Wales and Northern Ireland a partnership is not a separate legal entity distinct from the partners in the way that a company is from its shareholders (and the partners are not protected by limited liability). In Scotland however, partnerships are distinct legal entities.

LIMITED PARTNERSHIP (LP)

An LP typically has limited partners who, provided that they do not become involved in the management of the business, will not have liability for the debts and obligations of the firm. The limited partnership must also have at least one general partner who manages the business and bears unlimited liability to creditors. The general partner may, and generally will, be an entity such as a company which itself has limited liability.

Because of the limited liability and various tax benefits, LPs are a popular way to organise private equity investment. The investors - mostly pension funds and other big institutional investors - are limited partners, while the private equity firm managing the money is the general partner.

LIMITED LIABILITY PARTNERSHIP (LLP)

Created by the Limited Liability Partnerships Act 2000, LLPs are a combination of partnerships and limited liability companies.

Like limited liability companies, LLPs have a separate legal personality from their members but they are 'tax transparent', like partnerships. This means that the LLPs do not pay corporation tax. Income or gains are distributed to their partners, who then pay tax on it. LLPs are commonly used by accountants and lawyers.

The majority of LLPs are set up as normal business operations but a 2013 investigation by Private Eye magazine argued that the LLP structure and the lack of regulation around it has helped make Britain "the capital of corporate crime" by making it easier to hide illicit activities such as money-laundering.

COMMUNITY INTEREST COMPANY (CIC)

Created by the Companies (Audit, Investigations and Community Enterprise) Act 2004, a CIC is a special type of limited company which is meant to exist to benefit the community rather than private shareholders.

They can be limited by shares or guarantee. A company proposing to set up as a CIC must pass a 'community interest test'. To enable the regulator to decide if a company passes the test, the proposed CIC must provide a 'community interest statement'. A mandatory requirement in the articles of association of a CIC is the 'asset lock' which prevents the CIC selling its assets at undervalue and ensures that the CIC's assets are retained by the CIC and are used for the benefit of the community it was set up to serve.

INDUSTRIAL AND PROVIDENT SOCIETY (IPS)

An IPS is an incorporated organisation conducting an industry, business or trade, either as a co-operative run for the mutual benefit of its members, or for the benefit of the community. They are registered with the Financial Conduct Authority.

An IPS is controlled by all its members and must be run on the principle of one member, one vote.

These include countless small groups and societies, and larger ones such as housing associations. Many credit unions and building societies were set up as Industrial and Provident Societies but now have their own specific legislation.

TRUST

A trust is a legal arrangement where one or more 'trustees' are made legally responsible for holding assets such as land, money, buildings or shares that are placed in trust for one or more 'beneficiaries'. The trustees are responsible for managing the trust.

Trusts can be used for a range of purposes: by families to pass on assets through generations, for pension schemes, or for charitable purposes, where the beneficiaries will be a specified group of people in society. However, because often only the name of the trustee is disclosed publicly, they can also be used to shield people's finances from public scrutiny and to hide criminal activities such as tax evasion and money laundering.

A **unit trust** is a form of collective investment constituted under a trust deed. Unit trusts are highly regulated in most jurisdictions.

Note that so-called **investment trusts** are not actually trusts at all but incorporated companies. Investment trusts issue a fixed number of shares when they launch, which are then bought by investors. A professional fund manager then invests that money in the shares of other companies. A **mutual fund** is just one form of investment trust. '**Investment fund**' is often used synonymously with 'investment trust'.

CHARITIES

A charity is not a legal form but a status conferred on a not-for-profit organisation whose purposes are to provide a 'public benefit' and who fall under the charity criteria set by the Charities Act 2006. Such organisations can take a number of different legal forms, including associations, trusts and companies limited by guarantee. They are regulated by the Charity Commission of England and Wales, the Charity Commission of Northern Ireland and the Office of the Scottish Charity Regulator.

Don't assume that because an organisation has charitable status its behaviour will necessarily be ethical: there are all sorts of dodgy charities around.

OWNERSHIP AND SUBSIDIARIES

The fundamentals of company ownership are relatively easy to understand: whoever owns the shares in the company owns the company. But shareholders can be companies as well as people. If one company buys another for example, the buyer may simply run the company it has acquired as its owner and shareholder, rather than changing the direct ownership of all its possessions and operations.

When the retailing company Arcadia bought British Home Stores (BHS) in 2010 for example, it kept BHS going as a separate company that it owned all the shares of, rather than changing the direct ownership of all the possessions and operations. As Figure 1 shows, Arcadia also runs TopShop, Dorothy Perkins, Miss Selfridge, and Burton, among others, as subsidiary companies.

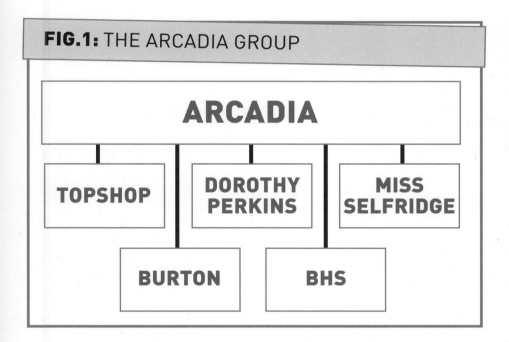

FIG.1: THE ARCADIA GROUP

ARCADIA

TOPSHOP | DOROTHY PERKINS | MISS SELFRIDGE

BURTON | BHS

The directors of a company may also decide to create subsidiaries to take care of certain parts of its everyday operations.

If they go to do business in a new country, they may set up a subsidiary that is registered in that country, with its own offices and staff. Marks and Spencer (Ireland) Limited, Marks and Spencer Czech Republic and Marks and Spencer (Asia Pacific) Limited are M&S subsidiaries selling its products in Ireland, Czech Republic and Hong Kong respectively, for example.

Sometimes, you'll find there's a chain of subsidiary companies. Have a look at the structure of the Yorkshire Water group (see figure 2). The 'operating' company – i.e. the one that hires the staff and owns the pipes that make water come out of Yorkshire taps – is Yorkshire Water Services Limited.

Its ultimate owners – HSBC bank and British, American and Singaporean investment funds – own it through a string of companies, which each own the shares of the company 'below' them in the chain. They each perform various financial or administrative functions, which, for legal or accounting reasons, the Yorkshire Water directors and accountants have decided it is best to do through a separate company. Companies like this are known as 'non-operating' companies as they don't actually produce or sell anything themselves. They are all run from the same office, share directors and employ few – if any – staff.

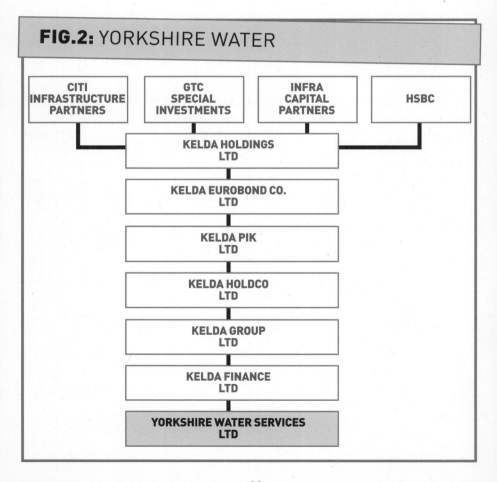

FIG.2: YORKSHIRE WATER

As a rule, the bigger the company, the more subsidiaries it will have. Marks and Spencer and the Arcadia group both have more than fifty, for example. Some of these may serve certain questionable purposes. Arcadia is owned through Jersey-registered companies by Cristina Green, the wife of Arcadia CEO Philip Green, and a resident of income-tax free Monaco, which helps keep the family's tax bills down. But most will probably just be playing some kind of administrative purpose. Be aware of the

> **FRANCHISING**: When one company or individual uses the business model and brand of another, it is operating as a franchise. Many McDonald's stores, for example, are run by individuals, who pay a royalty fee for using the McDonald's brand and management fees to the McDonald's corporation.

various subsidiaries but don't worry about understanding exactly why they've all been set up – chances are only a few of the company's accountants really know what they're all there for.

And don't be surprised to find companies listed as 'dormant', or that don't appear to do anything at all. They may have long ago performed whatever function they were originally set up for but it takes much more effort to eradicate a company than it does to create one.

In general, you can treat companies as if they are a single entity when they are all owned and controlled from the same source, and treat the owner as responsible for the actions of all the companies in the ownership chain (see page 53 for finding out the effect of the subsidiaries on a company's accounts).

As we saw with the Yorkshire Water example, many companies exist to make money from buying and selling the shares of other companies. Many of the largest shareholders in big companies are so-called institutional investors – banks, pensions and investment funds that pool people's money together.

This is especially true of publicly-quoted companies. Look at the list of Facebook's ten biggest shareholders as of the end of 2012:

1. Mark Zuckerberg   64.97%
2. Duston Moskovitz   8.30%
3. Eduardo Saverin   6.30%
4. FMR LLC via its funds   3.23%
5. Vanguard Group Inc via its funds   2.39%
6. Blackrock Inc, via its funds   1.81%
7. T Rowe Price Group Inc, via its funds   1.75%
8. Valiant Capital Management LP, via its funds   1.61%
9. Elevation Partners LP   1.50%
10. Invesco Ltd, via its funds   1.48%

Mark Zuckerberg has kept hold of 65% of the shares, and two other co-founders of the website are the next two biggest shareholders. But after them it's all investment funds.

Facebook is relatively new, and the longer companies shares are bought and sold, the more diversified their ownership tends to get. Take the shareholders of notorious outsourcing company G4S for the same date:

1. Invesco Ltd	16.04%
2. Prudential Plc via its funds	6.33%
3. Cevian Capital II GP Ltd	5.11%
4. Vidacos Nominees Ltd	5.11%
5. Affiliated Managers Group Inc via its funds	5.08%
6. Tweedy, Browne Global Value Fund	5.06%
7. M&G Investment Funds (1)	5.04%
8. BPCE SA via its funds	4.98%
9. Harris Associates LP	4.93%
10. Blackrock Inc via its funds	4.72%

All of its biggest shareholders are investment funds – who will each be managing the money of thousands of individuals. Often the people whose money the funds are investing don't know where it is going. Further down the list of G4S shareholders, for example, are the pension funds of public-sector workers from West Yorkshire and Wisconsin.

Many of them were surprised to learn, when told by campaigners protesting against G4S, that their pensions were invested in a company accused of manslaughter, mistreating their workers and cost-cutting in the public services they had taken over.

See section 3.1 for how to find out who a company's shareholders are.

FUNDS AND VOTING: When institutional investors own shares in a company they have voting rights, just like normal shareholders. However, it is usually the people who manage these funds that exercise the voting rights, not the people whose money is in the fund.

MAKING A PROFIT

Put simply, companies grow and make profits by selling goods or services for more than they spend making them.

As a general rule of thumb, the less companies can pay for things like staff, supplies, rent and tax, and the more they can charge customers for the products and services they make, the more profit they will make.

There are a variety of constraints that may hamper a company's attempts to make a profit, and it's good to keep them in mind when trying to work out the pressures on a company.

They include:

☐ Competition from other companies;

☐ Increased cost of supplies or raw materials;

☐ Reputation or 'brand';

☐ External economic factors such as rising interest rates or inflation, or a general decline in consumer spending;

☐ Regulations and state support, for example through subsidies or tariffs (hence many multinationals having ex-ministers or civil servants on their boards);

☐ Workers demanding and organising for better pay, benefits and working conditions;

☐ Negative public perception of their particular company, its activities or type of business or sector;

☐ Boycotts, protests or other resistance to their activities

In addition, there are two important qualifications that directors have to keep in mind while trying to increase the company's profits:

BALANCING LONG-TERM OR SHORT-TERM GAINS

The timeframe in which they're looking to make a profit matters. If a company increases the prices of its products, it may make it some short-term gains, but it may lose customers in the future, reducing its long-term profits, for example.

Equally, increased investment may hurt profits in the short-term, but bolster them in the long-term.

The terms under which people have invested their money in the company can influence how the directors run the business in this regard.

Shareholders in start-up companies are often tolerant of the losses they make in their early years, as they expect the future rewards to be worth the wait. Investors in bigger, established companies, however, may want a quicker return on their investment.

Some lenders may waive interest payments for a year or postpone repayment of a loan if they think they are better off giving a company a few more years to become more stable.

Others will insist on a full repayment on time, even if it means forcing the company into liquidation.

LIQUIDITY/CASH FLOW

While doing everything they can to increase the company's profits, directors also have to make sure it can pay its bills and running expenses. In the jargon, this is called liquidity. A company that doesn't have enough cash to pay its bills is said to be illiquid.

PROFITS AND WAGES: If the company you're working for says it can't afford to increase your wages, find out how much profit it is making. If you find it is posting consistently good profits - and it has enough cash - you could use this information to back-up demands for a pay rise. Those profits are being made on the back of the staff's work after all. See section 2.6 for how to find out how much profit a company is making and how much cash it has.

Not having enough cash is the number one reason why companies become insolvent and go under.

COMPANY FINANCING

Before companies can start trying to sell their products, they first need to produce them. To do this, they need things like equipment, property, and cash to pay workers and suppliers. The money they need for this is known as **capital**. Knowing where a company gets this from can help you understand their financial strengths and weaknesses, show who is profiting from its activities, and what claims they have on it.

DEBT AND EQUITY

Let's say two friends decide to set up a cake shop. They see it as an investment that they want to make money from, and possibly sell on in the future, so they decide to incorporate it as a limited company, which they both have one share in.

> **CAPITAL MEANINGS**: Confusingly, capital is sometimes used synonymously with equity, especially for banks. Capital investment, on the other hand, usually means investment in things that will be owned and used for a long period of time, like buildings, vehicles or machinery, rather than short-term costs like paying wages or bills.

The cake shop then becomes a legally separate entity from both of them. As the two friends want to work there themselves, they make themselves directors.

They've already got the recipes for the cakes but before they can make and sell them, they need to buy a building to do that from, an oven to cook them in, a van to deliver them with, then flour, fruit and all the other ingredients they need to make them.

There are two ways the new company can get the capital it needs to get started:

1. The two friends can invest their own money.
2. The company can borrow money, which will probably mean they will have to promise to pay the money back by a certain date, and in the meantime to pay a certain amount of interest every year to the lender.

If the company borrows the money, it would also have to agree that, in the event it can't pay back the money, the lender would have a claim to an equivalent amount of the cake shop's possessions and business.

> **SECURED OR UNSECURED**: Loans made with collateral are called secured. Those without are called unsecured. Paying interest on borrowings is often described as financing or servicing debt.

If, for example, the company takes a mortgage from a bank to buy a building to operate from, the bank would probably demand the building as 'collateral'.

Whoever the company is in debt to therefore has a claim on a proportion of what the company has. Legally, the friends' shares entitle them each to half of what the company is worth or, put another way, how much it has left after it has paid off its debts. In corporate finance terms, the difference between what a company owns and what it owes – or what the company is worth to its shareholders – is known as its equity.

This will change over time depending on how profitable the cake shop is. If the cake shop sells its cakes for more than it cost to make them, the amount of equity the two friends have a claim to will increase. However, let's say the oven catches fire and it's not insured. The company has lost a valuable possession, its debts haven't changed, so the equity the friends have a claim to would decrease. See Figure 3 for an example involving buying a house.

In general, the more equity a company has compared to its debt, the more financially stable it is. Companies are contractually obliged to pay interest payments whether or not they are profitable, whereas they can only pay dividends to shareholders if they are profitable, and even then the shareholders may decide not to take them (see below). In addition, large amounts of debt make the company far more exposed to external economic changes such as interest rate rises. Companies that have large amounts of debt and relatively little equity are said to have a high **debt to equity ratio**, or to be highly **geared** or **leveraged**. See section 2.6 to find out how much debt and equity a company has.

Note that both shareholders and lenders are **investors** in the company: they are both putting money into it for a return.

DIVIDENDS

If the cake shop makes a profit, the friends can choose to take out some or all of it out of the company straight away. These pay-outs are called dividends.

They could also choose to leave some or all of it in the business. What they do depends on how they want to expand the business. If they want to keep expanding it and don't desperately need or desire cash themselves, they may leave the money in so it can be invested elsewhere in the business. If it is invested well, the company's equity will increase, as will

> **NOT-FOR-PROFITS**: If not-for-profit companies sell their products or services for more than they cost to produce, what they make is called a surplus rather than a profit. This surplus stays in the company as there are no shareholders to distribute it to. If the cake shop was not-for-profit, the two friends could still have paid themselves a salary, but they wouldn't be able to receive dividends or make a profit from its sale. There are still opportunities for individual enrichment in not-for-profits of course, with some directors of the bigger UK charities and housing associations, among others, earning corporate-level salaries.

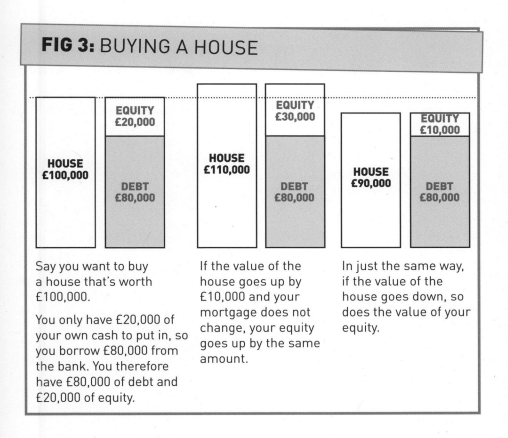

FIG 3: BUYING A HOUSE

Say you want to buy a house that's worth £100,000.

You only have £20,000 of your own cash to put in, so you borrow £80,000 from the bank. You therefore have £80,000 of debt and £20,000 of equity.

If the value of the house goes up by £10,000 and your mortgage does not change, your equity goes up by the same amount.

In just the same way, if the value of the house goes down, so does the value of your equity.

the value of their shares, meaning they can sell them for more in the future. See page 52 for how to find how much shareholders have received in dividends in a year.

EXPANSION

At this stage of the cake shop's life, its behaviour is determined by the two friends, within any constraints set by the terms of the bank loans. But this can soon change. Let's say the friends' cake recipe turns out to be a real winner and they want to set up another branch. However, they don't have enough money yet, so they need to find some outside investment.

Two local investors come along and say they'll put in enough money to buy a building for the new shop in return for a share in the company each. The two friends decide they'd rather the company take this money than take out another loan with the bank as they don't want to pay the bank's interest rates every year. Therefore, they authorise the company to issue two more shares. The two friends now only have a claim to a quarter of the company's equity each, but they've decided that the extra earnings to be made through the new shop is worth losing a proportion of their claim to, and control over, the business.

GOING PUBLIC

The corporate structure gives companies the potential for enormous growth if they can attract the investment. As companies get bigger, the amount of investors who want to buy their shares increases significantly.

Publicly-listing shares greatly increases the amount of potential shareholders that companies can attract, from banks and hedge funds buying shares just to make a quick profit by selling them on the same day, to campaigners buying a single share to protest at the AGM.

Going public often enables companies to grow faster and further, though it also brings increased regulation and can expose companies to the vagaries and hysteria of the financial world.

BONDS

The bigger the company, the more investors there are that want it to borrow from them. Instead of taking loans from the local bank, big companies can 'issue debt' in the form of multi-million pound bonds.

A **bond** is basically just an I.O.U. that sets out the terms by which the company will pay back the money it is borrowing, specifying the rate of interest (or 'coupon') it will pay and when it will pay the original sum (the 'principal') back to whoever 'buys' the bond (the 'bondholder').

Often, companies will 'list' bonds on a public exchange so that they increase the pool of people they can get money from.

Governments also issue bonds as a way of raising finance. The Bank of England

FLOATATIONS: When companies 'go public', or 'float' on a stock market (through what's known as an Initial Public Offering) they will usually issue a certain amount of new shares. The money paid for those shares will go straight into the company (as an equity investment).

After the initial offering, the shareholder, not the company, receives the money that they sell their shares for. The total value of a quoted company's issued shares is called its market capitalisation.

BUZZ WORDS: The business media likes to get excited about all sorts of bizarre financial shenanigans going on in and around a company. 'Derivatives' are used to 'hedge' loans, investors 'short' shares, while companies issue 'preferred shares'.

You can find out more about these terms with a quick web search. For a critical introduction, see Corporate Watch's Demystifying the Financial Sector guide.

has details of government bond rates, which you can use to compare with those of companies.

When someone buys a publicly-listed bond, they can then sell it to someone else, who is said to 'buy' the debt from them. This means it is often very difficult to work out exactly who a company owes money to. Often the companies themselves don't know all the people who own their bonds (though they should know who owns the largest shares). A company's accounts will usually tell you who gave the company a loan (see page 45) but the most you'll get on bonds is details of the companies or banks that performed insurance or administrative roles when the bond was issued. You could try contacting one of these companies, or the company that issued the bond, and ask if they've published the information anywhere. You could also try searching the web for the exact name of the bond. Some institutional investors publish details of their holdings, which may appear in a search.

Credit rating agencies - the biggest of which are Moody's, Standard & Poor's and Fitch - give these bonds ratings, which tend to determine the rates of interest companies have to pay out on them. Bonds rated from the highest rating - AAA - to BBB are classed as 'investment grade'. This means they are seen as more likely to be repaid and are therefore a safer investment. As a result, companies that issue investment grade bonds have to pay relatively lower interest rates to attract investors to buy them. Anything below BBB is known as a 'junk' bond, and is seen as more risky. The companies issuing the bonds therefore have to pay more interest to attract investors.

You might find the interest rates on some bonds or loans are described as being + a certain rate. This just means that the rate specified will be added to the interest paid out. If the interest is described as 3% + RPI, for example, the interest paid out each year will be 3% of the bond's value plus whatever the Retail Prices Index - a common measure of inflation - is at the time. This is popular as a way of guarding against the effects of inflation.

But even at this scale, the basic principles of corporate finance are still the same. Just like the cake shop, big companies are trying to sell their products for more than it costs to make them, and they can get any extra capital they need through equity or debt financing. And as with the bank and the cake shop, the lenders and bondholders know how much their claim on the company is worth by the value of the loan agreement they have made. The shareholders' claim changes according to how much is left after the company has paid all its debts.

COMPANY ACCOUNTS

Companies are required by law to publish a summary of their finances every year. These publications are called their annual accounts. They reveal more about a company's finances than any other public source. This section is an introduction to understanding them and explains the language they use and the principles they are based on.

See page 68 for how to get accounts from Companies House.

BALANCE SHEET

Also called the **Statement of Financial Position**, the balance sheet is the central document of a company's accounts – everything else relates to it.

It is a table showing a company's assets, liabilities and shareholder's equity on a particular day, and their value:

- ☐ Anything a company owns or is owed is called an **asset**
- ☐ Anything a company owes is called a **liability**

And, following on from section 2.5, the value of the **shareholder's equity** is the difference between the value of its assets and its liabilities (see page 35).

You can use the so-called '**balance sheet equation**' (accountants love equations) to work out the equity:

$$\text{Assets} - \text{liabilities} = \text{equity}$$

The balance sheet is presented with this equation in mind. Let's say Mrs Jones has the following assets and liabilities:

ASSETS		LIABILITIES	
House	£100,000	Mortgage	£80,000
Car	£10,000	Bank loan	£10,000
Computer	£400	Loan from sister	£4,000
Loan to brother	£5,000	Credit card debt	£1,000
Cash in the bank	£5,000	Electricity bill	£500
Cash in her wallet	£100	Student loan	£20,000

Her balance sheet would look like this:

BALANCE SHEET: MRS JONES

ASSETS	£
House	100,000
Car	10,000
Computer	400
Loan made to brother	5,000
Cash in the bank	5,000
Cash in wallet	100
Total assets	120,500
LIABILITIES	
Mortgage	(80,000)
Loan from bank to buy car	(10,000)
Loan from sister	(4,000)
Credit card debt	(1,000)
Outstanding electricity bill	(500)
Student loan	(20,000)
Total liabilities	(115,500)

Net assets		**£5,000**
EQUITY		**£5,000**

This clearly shows the difference between her assets and liabilities, and therefore the value of her equity. Note that:

- If a number in the accounts is in brackets it just means it's negative. Brackets are used because minus signs can be mistaken for dashes.
- Net just means the value of something after all relevant deductions have been made. In this case, net assets are assets minus liabilities.

The principles behind a company's balance sheet are the same. Let's say that the cake shop introduced in the last section has been going for a couple of years. Its balance sheet might look like that over the page. Notice that its liabilities include everything it owes (such as heating bills or payments to suppliers) to anyone –

not just the loans or bonds it owes to banks or investors. In accounts, anyone the company owes is called a 'creditor'.

Note the notes: look at a real set of accounts and you'll see small numbers between the descriptions and the values of items. These refer you to a note further back in the accounts, which will explain that item further. You should be reading these as you're going through the balance sheet and the other statements at the front of the accounts as they'll give extra details to help you understand each item. Get used to reading accounts with your thumbs and fingers keeping your place in a few pages at a time. See page 52 for more on the notes.

BALANCE SHEET: CAKE SHOP

ASSETS	£
Flour	400
Fruit	310
Cakes	1,100
Cash in till	1,200
Delivery van	3,800
Money in bank	7,000
Oven	950
Building	150,000
Money due from customers	600
Total assets	165,360
LIABILITIES	
Money due to flour mill	(500)
Money due to fruit growers	(600)
Mortgage	(150,000)
Wages	(1,900)
Utility bills	(900)
Business rates owed	(400)
Total Liabilities	(154,300)
Net assets	**11,060**
EQUITY	**11,060**

REGULATIONS

Over the years a common way for companies to present their accounts has developed, to allow investors and regulators to assess companies from around the world. They differ slightly from country to country, but all adhere to the broad criteria described here.

In the UK, accounting regulations – often called Generally Accepted Accounting Principles (GAAP) – are set by the Companies Act 2006 and the Financial Reporting Council, although all quoted companies and many bigger private companies use the International Financial Reporting Standards (IFRS), which are rules drawn up by the International Accounting Standards Board (IASB).

The most obvious differences are the names of some of the items in the accounts, which are noted throughout this section. The balance sheet, for example, is called the Statement of Financial Position in IFRS-compliant accounts. Where there are two names listed for the same item in this section, the first is the UK term, the second the IFRS.

There is no set day of the year that accounts have to be submitted for, though many follow the UK corporation tax year and draw them up for 31 March. However, the company has to stick to whatever day it picks. Companies have to get their accounts to Companies House within nine months of their accounting date.

If you see a company is late filing their accounts this might be a sign of financial difficulties or just disorganisation.

Most of the information in this section can also be used to understand the accounts of government bodies, charities and other non-corporate organisations.

CATEGORISING THE BALANCE SHEET

Most companies will have far too many individual assets and liabilities to list them all like we did with the cake shop. Instead, they will be grouped together into four main categories, based on whether the asset or liability will be held for less than a year (current) or more than a year (non–current):

☐ **Fixed assets:** assets that the company will have for a period of time longer than a year, for example property or machinery. For the cake shop, the building, oven and car would be fixed assets. These are also called **non–current assets** or **capital assets**.

□   **Current assets:** assets the company expects to sell or dispose of within a year, for example stock or money owed from customers. For the cake shop, these would be flour, fruit, cakes, cash in the till and money in the bank, unless it was a long-term savings account not readily accessible.

□   **Creditors – amount falling due within one year:** liabilities that the company expects to pay within a year, for example utility bills or money owed to suppliers. Also called **current liabilities**.

□   **Creditors – amount falling due after one year:** liabilities that the company expects to pay after a year, for example long-term bank loans, mortgages, bonds. Also called **non-current liabilities**.

Broken down into these categories, the cake shop's balance sheet would look like that on page 43 (real accounts also show the company's finances from the previous year's accounts to help compare and contrast).

Notice that the equity on the cake shop's balance sheet has been further broken down to show how the company came to that position.

We can see from this that the two friends decided to invest £7000 between them when the business started.

The retained earnings shows how much the cake shop has made over its life up to that point. We can see that the cake shop lost money – £900 – in its first year. In the second year, its assets increased by more than its liabilities to increase its total equity to £11060. As its retained earnings increased from –£900 to £4,060 we can work out that it must have made a profit of £4960, assuming it didn't pay out any dividends (see the Tesco case study on page 56 for the effects of this).

NEGATIVE EQUITY: If a company has more liabilities than assets, it is said to be in negative equity. This affects individuals too. After the financial crash for example, a lot of people found themselves in negative equity, after their homes sharply declined in value, often to below the amount of their outstanding mortgages, making their possessions worth less than their debts.

Remember that the figures on the cake shop's balance sheet relate to the financial situation of the company on two particular days – 31 March 2011 and 2012. We know from this that the stock of flour, fruit and cakes, and the money owed to suppliers and staff on the two days in question have all increased over the year, and that the net result of that has been a profit. But we don't know from the balance sheet the total amount of flour and fruit bought or cakes sold, or the total amount paid to the flour mill, fruit growers or staff. We only know the net result of all the transactions over the year.

The balance sheet therefore doesn't break down how the cake shop made that profit – it doesn't tell us about the company's total revenue or expenditure over the course of the year. That is what the profit and loss account is for (see below).

BALANCE SHEET: CAKE SHOP

	31.3.2012 £	31.3.2011 £
FIXED ASSETS		
Delivery van	3,800	4,000
Oven	950	1,000
Building	150,000	150,000
	154,750	**155,000**
CURRENT ASSETS		
Flour	400	150
Fruit	310	150
Cakes	1,100	450
Money owed by customers	600	200
Cash in till	1,200	500
Money in bank	7,000	2,000
	10,610	**3,450**
CREDITORS: AMOUNT FALLING DUE WITHIN ONE YEAR		
Money due to flour mill	(500)	(180)
Money due to fruit growers	(600)	(120)
Wages	(1,900)	(1,500)
Utility bills	(900)	(350)
Business rates owed	(400)	(200)
	(4,300)	**(2,350)**
Net current assets	6,310	1,100
CREDITORS: AMOUNT FALLING DUE AFTER ONE YEAR		
Mortgage	(150,000)	(150,000)
Net assets	11,060	6,100
Shareholders' Equity		
Capital invested	7,000	7,000
Retained earnings	4,060	(900)
TOTAL EQUITY	**11,060**	**6,100**

Bigger companies have far too many assets and liabilities to list individually, so you'll normally find the main categories are further broken down on real balance sheets into those below.

This means you won't be able to understand them as intricately or as comprehensively as we could understand the cake shop, but you can usually still get a good picture of their situation.

FIXED ASSETS:

Tangible fixed assets: fixed assets you can touch – buildings, land, machinery and so on.

Intangible assets: assets that have no physical form but are considered valuable resources of the business, for example patents, trademarks or brand names. In most cases accounting standards do not allow intangible assets to be valued in accounts unless they have been purchased by a company. Google, for example, has some of the most profitable intellectual property around but if you look at its accounts you'll find relatively few intangible assets, because they haven't been bought or sold. This is to prevent companies inflating their balance sheets at will.

'Goodwill' is an intangible asset that shows the difference between the amount a company paid to acquire another company, and the 'book value' of the assets of the company it bought. If Company A pays £50,000 to buy Company B, for example, but Company B's accounts say its assets are only worth £30,000, Company A will 'book' the remaining £20,000 as

WORKING CAPITAL: Working capital is a measure of a company's short-term financial strength and efficiency. It is calculated by deducting current liabilities from current assets. You'll see that most balance sheets are laid out to show this calculation.

The working capital ratio is worked out by dividing current assets by current liabilities.

If current liabilities are higher than assets, that means it may have problems paying off short-term debts, while a consistently high working capital ratio may be a sign it's not collecting money from customers very well.

goodwill in its accounts.

Goodwill is then depreciated over its useful economic life much like a piece of equipment (see page 47), except that the depreciation is called "amortisation".

How companies account for goodwill and intangible assets in general is too complicated to go into here. Check an accountancy textbook in your local library for more information.

Investments: any assets not used directly in the operation of a company's business – for example, shares in other companies that aren't part of the corporate group. If the investments are expected to be sold within the year, they would be classed as a current asset.

CURRENT ASSETS:

Stock/Inventory: a company's stock of unsold products, raw materials and other goods used in production.

Cash: in accounts, cash means any money the company can access quickly to pay people, so not necessarily just what the company has in physical notes or coins.

Assuming the cake shop's bank account was easily-accessible it would count as cash. If, however, it had a long term savings account that it couldn't access for a few years, this wouldn't be cash but would be classed as an investment.

Trade and other debtors/receivables: Money owed from customers or anyone else classed as a 'debtor' that the company expects will pay within a year.

This can also include prepaid expenses – expenses that the company has paid in advance of receiving the services.

CURRENT LIABILITIES:

Trade and other creditors/payables: money owed to suppliers (called vendors under IFRS regulations) and any other 'creditors' the company expects to pay within a year, which have already been delivered and invoiced to the company, but not yet paid for.

This can also include unearned revenue/deferred income – cash the company has received in advance of providing goods or services (the company therefore recognises the goods or service it owes as a liability).

Current tax liabilities: any tax the company will have to pay within a year, consisting of Corporation tax on profits for the year, VAT, and employment taxes. A **current tax asset** represents tax the company expects to receive in the year.

NON-CURRENT LIABILITIES:

Long-term borrowings: loans or bonds due to be paid back in more than one year. This, and the note attached to it, will give some details of lenders and the interest rates on the loans or bonds (see page 36).

Deferred tax liabilities: tax the company owes but will not pay this year. A deferred tax asset is tax the company expects to either receive back from the government, or be cancelled out by future tax it accrues. Deferred tax is complicated, but in broad terms it arises because companies like to 'even things out' between years – a bit like depreciation (see page 47).

Don't assume that large figures here are necessarily signs of aggressive tax avoidance. There are differences to the way expenditure is treated for tax, and the way it is treated for accounts, and this can give rise to large tax charges in one year, and low tax charges in another year. Deferred tax is a way of evening this out, so that the tax charge better reflects the actual profit for the year.

Provisions: if companies have assets they think may turn out to be worth less than currently recognised on the balance sheet, they can enter a provision for the amount they think they may eventually lose. Banks, for

COMPANY ACCOUNTS: KEY CONCEPTS

ACCRUALS

Say the cake shop from the last section agrees to sell a big batch of cakes to a hotel on a Monday, and at the same time agrees that the hotel will only pay when the cakes have been delivered on the Wednesday. In accounting terms, the revenue from the cakes has been earned on the Monday – that's when the deal has been made - so that's when it would be entered (or 'booked') into the accounts.

This is why the cake shop's balance sheet has an entry for 'money due from customers' – they have already agreed to buy the cakes, they just haven't paid for them yet.

This applies for expenses too. Say the cake shop receives an electricity bill on that same Monday. Even though the cake shop is not actually going to pay the bill until the week later, it would still book the bill amount as an expense for the Monday. Or take the wages item in the cake shop's accounts. This shows that staff are still to be paid for the work they've done.

Therefore:

- ☐ Revenue is recognised in a company's accounts when it is earned, not when the payment is actually received;
- ☐ Expenses are recognised in the accounts when they are incurred, not when they are paid.

THE GOING CONCERN ASSUMPTION

If a company folded shortly after its accounts had been drawn up, much of the information it had presented would have little practical basis. The company wouldn't be able to pay the debts listed in the accounts, and people that owed the company money may be be unlikely to pay, for example.

Directors therefore have to state in their report at the front of the accounts that they believe their company will be a 'going concern' until the next accounting year, and that is not about to stop trading. If that is in doubt, they should show why it is a going concern (for example, by saying the shareholders have committed to investing more in the business, or the lenders have postponed repayment of a loan). The auditors should also state if they think there's a risk over the company's going concern status, or if they disagree with the directors. Phrases like 'qualified opinion' or 'emphasis of matter' may suggest there's a problem.

DEPRECIATION

You may have noticed that the cake shop's van and oven decreased in value over the year. This is because of depreciation.

In accounting terms, this is recognising a reduction in the value of – or 'writing down' - an asset to reflect age and use. The more the cake shop uses the oven and the van, the less they will be worth.

If the van lasts, say, five years, then the effect of depreciation is to spread the cost of the van over the period in which it is used. If the van cost £5,000, then £1,000 depreciation would be taken off, and charged as an expense, every year.

Unfortunately for the cake shop, the bank loan it used to buy the oven and van does not depreciate in the same way!

Instead of a company deciding how much of an asset's value to write down each year, which creates opportunities for manipulation of the figures, and is against regulatory rules, assets are usually written down at the same rate each year (this is called straight-line depreciation).

BOOK VALUE AND MARKET VALUE

Of course, the cake shop could decide to sell the van after a few years and – because they've managed to keep it in pristine condition – get a better price than is shown in the accounts.

This is one example of how there may be a difference between the value of an asset in a company's accounts – its 'book value' – and how much it could be actually be sold for – the market value. If both sides are clued up with all the necessary information about the van, the market value will also be its fair value.

This applies to a company's overall worth. If a company is successful, its market value will usually be much higher than its book value in the accounts. Remember that investors buy shares in a company because of its potential future earnings, which may not be reflected by a company's present-day accounts.

The price that a company's shares are being bought and sold for may be very different to the figures you see in its accounts.

example, often enter provisions when they think they will not get back the full value of loans they have made.

EQUITY

Share capital: represents the total 'face' value of the shares a company has issued. This is a nominal amount that companies often set at £1 or another small amount. Plcs must have a minimum share capital of £50,000.

Share premium: the amount paid by shareholders to buy shares over and

> **SHARE VALUE**: Don't get confused by meagre-looking share capital or share premium amounts: because shares give you a share of the total equity and a company's future earnings, and because of the difference between book and market value, they are usually very different from what the shares are actually traded for.

above the face value of the shares. If the face value of a company's share is £1 but an investor paid £1,000 for it, the share premium would be £999.

Retained earnings: shows the 'net' earnings the company has made throughout its history. Increases or decreases according to the profit or loss made by the company in a particular year and how much has been paid out in dividends. Also called retained profit or the profit and loss account.

Big companies often now present a further **Statement of Changes in Equity** following the balance sheet to break down further the changes in the equity categories. This can be useful to see details of dividends to owners and other transactions with shareholders.

PROFIT AND LOSS ACCOUNT

A big company will make millions, perhaps billions, of individual sales and payments every year. Also called the **income statement**, the profit and loss account statement groups these into categories to show the total amount of sales the company has made, and how many expenses it has incurred. The difference between the two is the company's profit or loss for the year, and will relate to the profit and loss account on the balance sheet (see the examples on pages 42 and 56 for examples of how this works in practice).

The profit and loss account shows transactions made in the course of a company's everyday operations.

It does not include money a company has borrowed or that the shareholders have invested. This is classed as capital, not revenue, as it has not been earned in the normal run of business.

So-called capital expenditure – money spent on buying fixed assets – is also not included on the profit and loss account because these assets are not bought and sold, or 'turned over' in the normal run of business in the way that current assets are.

The profit and loss account will be at the front of the accounts, together with the balance sheet, of most medium to large companies. Go to page 59 to have a look at Tesco's profit and loss account (called the income statement because it is following IFRS rules).

In the UK, most profit and loss account statements will be broken down into four parts:

1. Gross profit = turnover – cost of sales
Turnover represents the amount made from all sales made during the accounting period (regardless of whether or not cash has been received yet – see page 46). Also called **income** or **revenue**.

Cost of sales represents the cost of making those sales. For a company like Tesco, this would include the cost of buying or making their products, running their shops and the wages of the staff working in the shops.

WHAT PROFIT TO LOOK AT: Which profit figure is most relevant will depend on what you're looking for. The gross profit tells you how profitable the company's basic business of making and selling whatever goods or services it offers is. Operating profit includes the cost of expenses necessary for the functioning of the business.

Profit before tax adds in the cost of the company's financing arrangements. A company's profit margin is worked out by dividing net income by revenue (so the profit margin of a company with net income of £10 and revenue of £100 would be 10%).

2. Operating profit = gross profit – operating expenses
Operating expenses include:
- ☐ **Distribution costs:** Packaging, postage and transport costs, for example.
- ☐ **Administrative expenses:** Money spent on the general running of a business or organisation, rather than on producing goods or selling services. For a supermarket like Tesco, this would include costs incurred in, say, the human resources and accounting departments but not their factories or shops.
- ☐ **Depreciation:** Recognises the decrease in an asset's value over its life (see page 47).
- ☐ **Amortisation:** Like depreciation but for intangible assets (see page 44).
- ☐ **Impairment:** A reduction of the value of an asset but not one that occurs in a predictable way like depreciation. A piece of machinery that has broken and so no longer has an economic use will be written down or 'impaired' to its scrap value, for example. If a bank realises a customer is unlikely to pay back a loan – either in full or in part – it will recognise the money it would lose from this as an impairment expense in the income statement (while reducing the value of its loans in its balance sheet accordingly). Years after the credit crunch, impairments remain a common feature of many banks' income statements.

3. Profit before tax = operating profit + other income – financing costs

☐ **Financing costs**: Money the company is paying in interest on the loans or bonds it has.

☐ **Other income (or non-operating income):** Any other income the company has made – usually interest or dividends it has received on investments or from subsidiary companies.

4. Profit for the year = profit before tax – corporation tax

(Note the corporation tax figure here is the tax the company has incurred for the year, not how much it has actually paid – this is found in the cash flow statement, below.)

The accounts of quoted companies will usually tell you the 'earnings per share' – how much each share has increased in (book) value over the year.

The accounts may say a proportion of the profit is attributable to a minority interest. This refers to the portion of a company's equity that is not owned by the parent company. This will be less than 50% of its shares.

Big companies often include a **statement of comprehensive income** or

RETURN ON EQUITY: the business media and a company's annual report will often talk about a company's return on equity. It is a key measure of a company's profitability and is the most common way for shareholders to assess how much of a return they're getting on their investment.

It is calculated as a percentage by dividing a company's profit after tax with the total value of the shareholder's equity.

SMALL FIRMS: accounting regulations often do not require smaller companies to present income or cash flow statements but you can still get some idea of their profits by looking at the change in the retained profit in the balance sheet from the previous to current year, although try to check if dividends have been paid, as they are also taken from the retained earnings (see pages 42 and 56 for examples of this).

recognised gains and losses at the front of the accounts with the income statement. This includes any gains or losses that affect shareholders' equity but are not part of the income statement. It includes things like gains or losses in the value of the company's pension scheme, currency translation, or certain investments, depending on the standards applied by the relevant accounting jurisdiction. These should really all be included in the income statement as they affect a company's retained profit. But because they are all very changeable and volatile – and because companies want to show consistent profits on their income statements – regulators allow them to be grouped together separately.

COOKING THE BOOKS

When to book revenue and expenses often isn't an exact science and the ambiguity can be used to manipulate results according to the needs of the company. As one example of many, technology firm Hewlett-Packard has recently concluded that Autonomy, the British software company it bought for more than £7.1bn, made 80% less profits than originally stated in its accounts, due to accounting irregularities by the former management team. You may spot signs of dodgy accounting like this – if the operating profit and operating cash flow are significantly different over a period of years for example – but, even if you're an expert, this can be very hard to spot just from the published accounts. The auditors are meant to check for this so always read their report at the front of the accounts to see if they raise any doubt (although there are many cases - that of Enron most famously - of auditors not doing their job as stringently as they might).

CASH FLOW STATEMENT

The cash flow statement tells you how much cash the company has spent or received over the accounting period and relates to the cash asset on the balance sheet. Unlike the profit and loss statement, this includes cash spent or received through capital expenditure (the buying or selling of fixed assets) and financing. Remember that cash in accounts means any money the company can access quickly to pay people, and that running out of cash is the most common reason that companies go out of business (see pages 23 and 32). Common categories that a company's cash transactions are grouped into on the cash flow statement include:

☐ **Operating activities:** net cash received from a company's day-to-day operations. Because of the accruals basis of accounting, cash from operating activities is unlikely to be the same as the operating profit in the income statement. Over the whole life of the company however, they should always match up.

☐ **Capital expenditure:** cash from the buying and selling of fixed assets.

☐ **Returns on investments** or **servicing of financing:** cash paid out as interest on the company's debt, or cash it has received in dividends or interest from shares it owns or loans it has made.

☐ **Taxation:** cash paid out as tax. Note that the cash flow statement shows cash paid for the previous period's tax bill. This won't be the same as the tax figure on the income statement, which shows a company's tax charge from its activities for the accounting period just finished. These figures can be quite different so be careful that you don't mix them up. If this is a positive amount, it is because the company has received money back from the government as a tax credit.

☐ **Dividends paid:** dividends paid out to shareholders.

☐ **Financing:** cash received from the raising of funds to run the business, for example in return for new shares or bonds issued or new loans taken.

NOTES TO THE ACCOUNTS

As explained above, the notes are an integral part of the accounts and most should be read in tandem with the primary statements.

However, some notes don't directly relate to the primary statements but still contain lots of important details. These include:

ACCOUNTING POLICIES

Usually the first or second note in the accounts, this tells you the particular criteria the company is using to draw up its accounts. It will include details of how they are calculating depreciation of assets, and if the accounts are consolidated, for example. It will also tell you how – if at all – the company is revaluing any of its assets.

SEGMENTAL ANALYSIS

Some companies will break down their revenue and expenditure across their operations – for example by country or sector.

However, most of the time these do not disclose anything like the amount of information a full set of accounts would for each set of operations in each different area.

EMPLOYEES AND STAFF COSTS

This will tell you total numbers of employees, and their total wages and benefits paid. Big companies will often include social security costs. Some companies, and many public sector organisations, use this note to provide a detailed breakdown of the different levels of staff pay, and an overall average. This information may also be contained in their annual report, if they produce one (see page 62).

DIRECTORS' PAY

This should at least give you the details of what the highest paid director is making. Most big, public companies will have a much more detailed breakdown, though this will often be in their annual reports (see page 62). Directors often receive bonuses and pension contributions in addition to their salary, so be careful you don't mix up the different figures.

DIVIDENDS

This note explains how much was paid out to shareholders over the past year and how much has been agreed to be paid out over the next year.

Be careful not to confuse the dividends that have been paid out in the accounting year, and the dividends proposed for the upcoming year (based on this year's results).

For quoted companies, the directors will propose an amount to be paid out and shareholders will vote on whether to accept it. If the accounts are prepared before the vote has been taken, they will usually show how much has been proposed to be paid.

If you're not sure, check the cash flow statement to confirm how much was paid out last year.

See page 34 for an explanation of dividends.

ACCOUNTS: CONSOLIDATED OR COMPANY?

For accounting purposes, companies are treated as being part of the same group when they are all ultimately owned and controlled by the same source, and are run as if they were a single economic entity.

As shown on page 28, the parent company of the Yorkshire Water group is Kelda Holdings Limited. That is owned by four different shareholders – banks and investment companies that have separate economic interests and sources of control. They are therefore not classed as being part of the Yorkshire Water group, which includes Kelda Holdings Limited and all the companies beneath it in the chain.

You should always be sure if you're looking at the accounts of an individual company, or the 'consolidated' accounts of the whole group. Each individual subsidiary in the group will have its own accounts, detailing its own finances. The consolidated accounts merge all of these different accounts together, and cancel out all of the transactions between the companies in the group (they 'net out' the intra-group transactions, in the jargon).

To get your head round this, imagine how the finances of the family below would look if they were 'consolidated' together:

☐   A couple have a house worth £150,000 with a £130,000 mortgage still to pay off. They have £5,000 of credit card debts and they have lent their daughter £20,000.

☐   Their parents own a house worth £200,000 and have no debts.

☐   Their daughter owes £10,000 in gambling debts incurred over the last month and owes her parents £20,000 from the debts she ran up last year.

The 'consolidated' finances of the family as a whole would show:

☐   They own property worth £350,000 (couple's house + parents' house)

☐   They owe debts of £145,000 (couple's mortgage, credit card debt + daughter's gambling debts).

Clearly this is very different from any of their individual situations, which are obscured by the consolidation. An outside observer wouldn't know that the extent of the daughter's financial problems for example, because the loan between the couple and their daughter wouldn't show up. ▸▸

ACCOUNTS: CONSOLIDATED OR COMPANY? CONTINUED

While you need to look at the consolidated accounts to get a picture of a company's finances as a whole, they may not tell you enough about the financial flows between the individual companies in the group enough. If you want to look at how much money a company made overall last year, for example, you'd look at the consolidated accounts. To know what it is making in each area it's working in, you need to get the accounts of the relevant subsidiary. But this isn't always easy. There are regulatory exemptions that allow companies not to disclose their 'intra-group transactions in certain circumstances, while some jurisdictions – such as Jersey, Switzerland, Cayman Islands and other tax havens - don't require companies to even publish accounts. This allows companies to shift profits 'offshore' in ways that don't show up in the group accounts and can make it very hard to find exactly where the money is, and enabling tax avoidance and other financial sleights of hand.

However, even if the parent company is registered offshore, you are still entitled to see its consolidated accounts if there are UK companies in the group of companies it is the head of. If the company does not publish these on its website, you can write to the company secretary, whose contact details should be listed at the end of the accounts, and request they send you a copy.

PENSIONS

This will show much credit or deficit the company's pension scheme for its employees is in.

How companies account for pensions is very complicated and this will often be a very long note.

Pensions can be very volatile and show significant deficits or credits that will get cancelled out the next year.

This may come from slight changes in the equations that the actuaries who plan the scheme have used – for example assuming people will live for six months longer than previously anticipated.

SUBSIDIARIES

A list of the company's subsidiaries – companies it owns more than 50% of the voting rights in – or at least all the major ones. This includes companies in the UK and around the world.

Companies that the parent owns between 20% to 50% of are called **associate companies**.

RELATED PARTY TRANSACTIONS

The Financial Reporting Council regulator deems two companies to be related when one has control over the other or they are both "subject to common control" from the same source.

In both consolidated and non-consolidated accounts, this note will show transactions between the company and its owners and any other commonly-owned companies. In an individual company's accounts this will also show transactions with companies in the same group.

Always check this note if you suspect a company is **avoiding tax** as this is where you'll find details of payments to any offshore companies the owners have that aren't part of the group, although, as explained on page 54, transactions with offshore companies within the group won't show up here (spotting tax avoidance is too big a subject to include in this handbook, but check the tax figures on the profit and loss and cash flow statements, and this note and the subsidiary note for any offshore companies to get an idea of whether there may be something to look into).

Transactions with directors are also included here, as are other companies the company owns or controls.

OWNERS

One of the last notes should tell you who owns the company. If it is part of a group, this will tell you the immediate parent company and, if you're lucky, the 'ultimate' owners of the group.

See page 65 for more on finding company owners.

POST BALANCE SHEET EVENTS

This will show any significant changes to the company's finances since the accounting period.

AUDITORS' AND DIRECTORS' REPORTS

Unlike a company's annual report, the accounts of all but the smallest companies' accounts have to be **audited**. An external, independent auditor is supposed to check the figures in the accounts are a 'true and fair' presentation of the company's finances. They have to give their opinion on the validity of the accounts in a report at the beginning. If they have any doubt they will express a "qualified opinion" or an "emphasis of matter". These are phrases to watch out for as they often suggest that the company is in some financial trouble.

Accounts also contain a **report by the directors** at the beginning. This is not audited and allows the directors to describe the company's operations and the business context to the results. It also includes other information such as **charitable** and **political donations**. It will be very short if the company combines its accounts with an annual report (see page 62).

FURTHER READING

Accounts Demystified: The Astonishingly Simple Guide to Accounting by Anthony Rice is an excellent and accessible introduction to understanding accounts. For more detailed guides, check your local library for accounting textbooks.

Investopedia, FT Lexicon and the Wikipedia websites all describe and explain the terms and concepts introduced here – and many more besides.

CASE STUDY: TESCO

As an example of the kind of things you can learn from accounts, let's have a look at the 2013 accounts of supermarket giant, Tesco. Get hold of the 2013 Tesco Plc annual report (you can download it for free from their website, or from Companies House, for £1), so you can look at the notes that there's not space to include here.

As this is a basic example, we just want to look at the company's overall finances, so we first need to check we're looking at the consolidated accounts.

The balance sheet, reproduced on the page opposite, is the cornerstone of the accounts, so let's start here. It's titled 'Group' so we know these are consolidated accounts, which, as we want to look at Tesco's overall finances, are the most suitable.

The '£m' at the top of each column means that all the figures are in millions (£'000s means thousands, and so on). The amounts are huge, and there are a lot more categories than were on our cake shop's balance sheet, but the principles are the same. The balance sheet equation still applies and the value of the assets (£37 billion non-current assets + £13bn current assets = £50bn) are the same as the total liabilities (£33bn) and shareholder's equity (£17bn) combined.

Now compare the 2013 figures with those of 2012. The value of Tesco's assets went down by about £700m while its liabilities increased by about £500m. As a result, the shareholder's equity decreased by £1.2bn, suggesting the company didn't have such a good year in 2013. The most obvious change is in the retained earnings, which went down by around £1.5bn.

The income statement (page 59) helps to explain what has happened to the retained earnings.* That shows Tesco's profitability did indeed take a hit, going down by more than £2bn and that Tesco made a loss of £1.2bn from what are called "discontinued operations". To find out what they are we need to go to note 7, which explains these are losses made from its botched US expansion.

However even without that loss, its profits from continuing operations also went down significantly (from £3.2bn to £1.4bn). The main reason for that looks like an increase in the cost of sales. Tesco's overall revenue actually increased in 2013, meaning it sold more goods. But the cost of producing

Group balance sheet

	23 February 2013 £m	25 February 2012 £m
Non-current assets		
Goodwill and other intangible assets	4,362	4,618
Property, plant and equipment	24,870	25,710
Investment property	2,001	1,991
Investments in joint ventures and associates	494	423
Other investments	818	1,526
Loans and advances to customers	2,465	1,901
Derivative financial instruments	1,965	1,726
Deferred tax assets	58	23
	37,033	37,918
Current assets		
Inventories	3,744	3,598
Trade and other receivables	2,525	2,657
Loans and advances to customers	3,094	2,502
Derivative financial instruments	58	41
Current tax assets	10	7
Short-term investments	522	1,243
Cash and cash equivalents	2,512	2,305
	12,465	12,353
Assets of the disposal group and non-current assets classified as held for sale	631	510
	13,096	12,863
Current liabilities		
Trade and other payables	(11,094)	(11,234)
Financial liabilities:		
Borrowings	(766)	(1,838)
Derivative financial instruments and other liabilities	(121)	(128)
Customer deposits and deposits by banks	(6,015)	(5,465)
Current tax liabilities	(519)	(416)
Provisions	(188)	(99)
	(18,703)	(19,180)
Liabilities of the disposal group classified as held for sale	(282)	(69)
Net current liabilities	(5,889)	(6,386)
Non-current liabilities		
Financial liabilities:		
Borrowings	(10,068)	(9,911)
Derivative financial instruments and other liabilities	(759)	(688)
Post-employment benefit obligations	(2,378)	(1,872)
Deferred tax liabilities	(1,006)	(1,160)
Provisions	(272)	(100)
	(14,483)	(13,731)
Net assets	16,661	17,801
Equity		
Share capital	403	402
Share premium	5,020	4,964
All other reserves	685	245
Retained earnings	10,535	12,164
Equity attributable to owners of the parent	16,643	17,775
Non-controlling interests	18	26
Total equity	16,661	17,801

CASE STUDY: TESCO

the goods it sold increased by £1.5bn (in the annual report released with these accounts, the CEO blames it on investment in its UK stores, the Eurozone crisis and legislation restricting opening hours in South Korea, Tesco's largest market outside the UK).

However, the company still made a profit, albeit a relatively meagre £120m. So why has the retained earnings on the balance sheet gone down by so much (by £1.2bn compared to a loss of £120m)?

To find out why, look at the statement of changes in equity on page 75 of the accounts (not reprinted here). This shows the main reason for the equity decline is a £1.2bn dividend payout to shareholders.

Dividends are taken straight out of the company's cash holdings and you can see the payout on the cash flow statement overleaf.* Tesco's assets therefore went down, and as there was no change in its liabilities, its equity went down too.

Tesco's directors know they haven't had a great year but they seem to be worried about keeping the shareholders onside, so have kept their dividends at the same level as previous, more profitable, years. This has weakened the company's overall financial stability, as equity has decreased in relation to debt, but the directors presumably believe they can get back to previous profit levels, and have decided they need to keep their investors sweet until then.

Tesco is hardly in financial trouble, but its accounts show it is having problems. It cannot keep paying out dividends like this if its profits don't go back up, meaning it may be at risk of losing some major investors.

A company's accounts then, can show vulnerabilities that may not otherwise be apparent.

* Don't worry about the Non-GAAP measure statement or the Reconciliation of net cash flow to movement in net debt note beneath the income statement and the cash flow statements respectively. They provide additional information that Tesco wants to show investors, and they are not part of the main statements.

Group income statement

Year ended 23 February 2013	52 weeks 2013 £m	52 weeks 2012 £m
Continuing operations		
Revenue	64,826	63,916
Cost of sales	(60,737)	(58,519)
Gross profit	4,089	5,397
Administrative expenses	(1,562)	(1,612)
Profits/losses arising on property-related items	(339)	397
Operating profit	2,188	4,182
Share of post-tax profits of joint ventures and associates	54	91
Finance income	177	176
Finance costs	(459)	(411)
Profit before tax	1,960	4,038
Taxation	(574)	(874)
Profit for the year from continuing operations	1,386	3,164
Discontinued operations		
Loss for the year from discontinued operations	(1,266)	(350)
Profit for the year	120	2,814
Attributable to:		
Owners of the parent	124	2,806
Non-controlling interests	(4)	8
	120	2,814
Earnings per share from continuing and discontinued operations		
Basic	1.54p	34.98p
Diluted	1.54p	34.88p
Earnings per share from continuing operations		
Basic	17.30p	39.35p
Diluted	17.30p	39.23p

Non-GAAP measure: underlying profit before tax		
	52 weeks 2013 £m	52 weeks 2012 £m
Profit before tax from continuing operations	1,960	4,038
Adjustments for:		
IAS 32 and IAS 39 'Financial Instruments' – fair value remeasurements	14	(44)
IAS 19 'Employee Benefits' – non-cash Group Income Statement charge for pensions	(56)	17
IAS 17 'Leases' – impact of annual uplifts in rent and rent-free periods	28	31
IFRS 3 'Business Combinations' – intangible asset amortisation charges and costs arising from acquisitions	19	22
IFRIC 13 'Customer Loyalty Programmes' – fair value of awards	28	17
Restructuring and other one-off costs		
Impairment of PPE and onerous lease provisions	895	–
Impairment of goodwill	495	–
Provision for customer redress	115	57
Other restructuring and one-off costs	51	11
Underlying profit before tax from continuing operations	3,549	4,149

CASE STUDY: TESCO

Group cash flow statement

Year ended 23 February 2013	52 weeks 2013 £m	52 weeks 2012 £m
Cash flows from operating activities		
Cash generated from operations	3,873	5,688
Interest paid	(457)	(531)
Corporation tax paid	(579)	(749)
Net cash generated from operating activities	2,837	4,408
Cash flows from investing activities		
Acquisition/disposal of subsidiaries, net of cash acquired/disposed	(72)	(65)
Proceeds from sale of joint ventures and associates	68	–
Proceeds from sale of property, plant and equipment, investment property and non-current assets classified as held for sale	1,351	1,141
Purchase of property, plant and equipment, investment property and non-current assets classified as held for sale	(2,619)	(3,374)
Purchase of intangible assets	(368)	(334)
Net (increase)/decrease in loans to joint ventures and associates	(43)	122
Investments in joint ventures and associates	(158)	(49)
Net proceeds from sale of/(investments in) short-term and other investments	1,427	(767)
Dividends received from joint ventures and associates	51	40
Interest received	85	103
Net cash used in investing activities	(278)	(3,183)
Cash flows from financing activities		
Proceeds from issue of ordinary share capital	57	69
Increase in borrowings	1,820	2,905
Repayment of borrowings	(3,022)	(2,720)
Repayment of obligations under finance leases	(32)	(45)
Purchase of non-controlling interests	(4)	(89)
Dividends paid to equity owners	(1,184)	(1,180)
Dividends paid to non-controlling interests	–	(3)
Own shares purchased	–	(303)
Net cash used in financing activities	(2,365)	(1,366)
Net increase/(decrease) in cash and cash equivalents	194	(141)
Cash and cash equivalents at beginning of the year	2,311	2,428
Effect of foreign exchange rate changes	26	24
Cash and cash equivalents including cash held in disposal group at the end of the year	2,531	2,311
Cash held in disposal group	(19)	(6)
Cash and cash equivalents at the end of the year	2,512	2,305

Reconciliation of net cash flow to movement in net debt note

Year ended 23 February 2013	52 weeks 2013 £m	52 weeks 2012 £m
Net increase/(decrease) in cash and cash equivalents	194	(141)
Elimination of net (increase)/decrease in Tesco Bank cash and cash equivalents	(475)	126
Investment in Tesco Bank	(45)	(112)
Debt acquired on acquisition	(1)	(98)
Net cash outflow to repay debt and lease financing	1,589	262
Dividend received from Tesco Bank	105	100
(Decrease)/increase in Retail short-term investments	(721)	221
Increase/(decrease) in Retail joint venture loan receivables	36	(122)
Other non-cash movements	(430)	(330)
Elimination of other Tesco Bank non-cash movements	(11)	46
Decrease/(increase) in net debt for the year	241	(48)
Opening net debt	(6,838)	(6,790)
Closing net debt	(6,597)	(6,838)

PART 3
SOURCES

COMPANIES

As well as speaking to the company and its workers directly (see sections 1.4 and 1.5), you can find a lot of useful information in the company's publications.

In general, the information that companies publish about themselves will be most useful for finding out details of their finances, staff and shareholders. Their reports and updates on their operations are unlikely to portray the company as anything other than squeaky clean.

ANNUAL REPORT

Many companies – and pretty much all big companies – produce an annual report together with their accounts, describing their activities over the previous year, including details of their operations and headline financial results. You can usually download the annual report for free from the company's website. The reports of the bigger multinationals describe their operations in different countries and a breakdown of their various **operations**, **worksites**, **staff numbers and pay**, and, usually, **directors' pay**. Some companies will also include a **corporate social responsibility (CSR) report** in their annual report, while some will release this separately (see the Corporate Watch report for a critical view of CSR).

Remember that these reports are intended to present the company in the best possible light in order to maintain investor and shareholder confidence. They are usually big, glossy publications, full of pictures of smiling people talking about how great the company is. Unlike the accounts, they are not audited.

WEBSITE

Companies' websites are becoming increasingly informative, and include most of the information in the annual report, plus news, history and press releases, as well as updated sections on senior staff and their operations. Most are expanding their **social media** profiles, so following their Twitter, Facebook, Youtube and other accounts can be a good way of keeping up to date with their announcements.

ACCOUNTS

Reading a company's annual accounts is the best way to find out how much money it has. They won't give you all the information you want but they're the best source available, short of speaking to the company's accountants.

Among many valuable nuggets of information, the two main things the accounts give you are:

- ☐ a snapshot of what the company owns and what it owes;
- ☐ details of its financial transactions over the last year, including how much profit it made, how much tax it paid, how much cash it has and how much it paid to its shareholders.

See section 2.6 for an introduction to reading and understanding company accounts.

You'll usually be able to download the accounts of bigger companies from their website. If not, you can get them from Companies House (see below).

The amount of information a company publishes in its accounts will depend on how big it is. Smaller companies are allowed to disclose much less information – often just a balance sheet, a basic income statement and a few notes. Disclosure requirements also differ according to the country the company is registered in. Some tax havens don't require companies to publish accounts.

INTERNAL DOCUMENTS

For obvious reasons, documents not intended for public viewing – for example memos, emails, presentations, strategy documents or evaluations – tend to be far more candid about the company and its operations.

Your best bet for getting these is from a member of staff who's annoyed at the company and sympathetic to what you're doing (see page 12). If you've got the time and inclination, you could even try to get a job with the company, though you'd have to be in it for the long haul to get access to really sensitive material (see page 13).

Update emails or newsletters that many companies send to their employees often include new details of recently awarded or completed contracts, site changes or new offices, staff and director changes and management/training/computer systems in the group (though you've often got to wade through a sewer of corporate speak to get to the good stuff).

Management accounts are produced for internal use, often a few times a year (as opposed to the publicly available statutory accounts that are produced annually). They are intended to inform decisions regarding the management of the company and will usually go into a lot more detail than statutory accounts, breaking revenue down by individual product line, or showing the cost and profits of individual sites, for example.

INVESTOR PRESENTATIONS

Publicly-listed companies and some private companies also produce investor presentations and updates for their shareholders and potential investors, which contain financial news and analysis. The information provided for shareholders may be more enlightening than that shared with the public so can be useful to have a look at.

You can usually find them in the Investor Relations section of a company's website, although they are often password-protected from the general public.

Buying a share should allow you to access this. It'll set you back a few quid but it may be worth it for the access it gives you. You'll have to do this through a stockbroker – either online or by phoning them up and screaming "BUY!" in your best banker voice.

ANNUAL GENERAL MEETING (AGM)

Buying a share also gets you an invitation to the company's AGM, where directors present updates on the previous year's activities and future plans. Votes are held to approve dividends, elect the board of directors and to approve their remuneration, as well as on certain other issues arising and resolutions. Emergency general meetings (EGMs) are held when a matter arises that cannot wait till the AGM. If you don't have a share but know someone who does, you can go as their 'proxy'. Otherwise, AGMs of larger companies are often covered by the mainstream media and the business media, so you can at least track any significant decisions or developments through them. You can also go along to identify the shareholders that are attending and try to talk to them.

REGULATORY NOTIFICATIONS

Publicly-listed companies are also required to submit a variety of regulatory notifications depending on the stock exchange their shares are listed on. For the London Stock Exchange (LSE) this includes half-yearly reports in addition to the annual accounts, profit expectations, significant changes to their financial structure, transactions with directors, and any proposals for mergers or acquisitions. You can normally download these from the LSE website, where you can also find the company's current, and historical, **share price**.

BOND PROSPECTUS

A bond prospectus produced by a company when issuing new debt to the market will likely be a big, dense document but it may contain information about a company's finances that you won't find in the accounts, as well as details of the terms of the bond (how much interest it will pay, what it is secured against and so on).

Many are publicly available and can be found through a web search using the exact name of the bond, as stated in the accounts (see page 37). Otherwise you'll have to ask the company for a copy or access the investor relations part of their website.

The business media and other business information sources provide lots of useful analysis of a company's finances. See section 3.5 for details.

CASE STUDY: Leaking Away – the financial costs of water privatisation

By trawling through the accounts of the 19 water and sewerage companies in England and Wales, Corporate Watch found:

- ☐ Almost one third of the money spent on water bills goes to banks and investors as interest and dividends.

- ☐ People are paying £2 billion more a year – or around £80 per household - than they would if the water and sewerage supply was publicly financed.

- ☐ The CEOs of the 19 water companies were paid almost £10m in salaries and other bonuses in 2012.'

- ☐ Six companies are avoiding millions of pounds in tax by routing profits through tax havens, using a regulatory loophole the government has chosen to keep open.

OWNERSHIP

If you want to find out who owns a **private limited company** (one with **Ltd** after its name – see page 24), first check the back of the accounts, which often contain details of the company's principal shareholder (see page 55).

ANNUAL RETURN

For details of all the shareholders, you need to get the Annual Return, which all companies are required to submit to Companies House. The Statement of Capital at the back of the annual return lists all the shareholders of a limited company and shows how many shares they each own.

If the company is part of a group the listed owner will be the immediate parent company within the group, rather than the ultimate parent company or shareholders. In this case, you'll have to get the annual return of that company, then the one that owns it, and so on. See section 2.3 to understand company ownership.

The annual returns of **publicly-listed companies (plcs)** do not contain shareholder details. You have to order a DVD-ROM for a list, which is updated every three years. However, since the requirements changed in 2009, plcs have only had to disclose the details of shareholders who have more than five percent of the company's shares. This has made it very hard to find out details of all the shareholders of publicly-listed companies.

SHARE REGISTER

The document you really want is the company's Share Register, which lists all the current shareholders. You can ask the company or its registrar (the company that administers the register) for a copy, but you have to have a 'proper purpose' for doing so and it's a legal offence to lie when describing why you need it. If you pass the proper purpose test, you'll have to pay to get a copy – more than £100 if it's a big multinational – or you can go down to the registrar's office to have a look at the register in person, although non-shareholders also have to pay for this. You can see it for free if you're a shareholder (though you'll still have to pay to get your own copy) but only if you do the proper purpose test.

For more information, see the briefing on this by the Institute of Chartered Secretaries & Administrators, available online. See page 75 for corporate databases that contain full lists of shareholders from publicly-quoted companies.

REGULATORY DISCLOSURES

The London Stock Exchange (LSE) requires disclosure of any major changes in share holdings (usually three percent or more). You can piece together a broad picture of a company's ownership by trawling through these in the market news section of the LSE website.

INSTITUTIONAL INVESTORS

Given that so-called institutional investors – banks, insurance companies, pension and other investment firms that pool the money of thousands of different investors – now own a significant amount of UK company shares (see section 2.3), you could see if they have invested in the company you're interested in.

If you want to find out what a particular pension or investment fund owns, go to the website of the company or organisation that is managing the fund and look for the accounts or investment portfolios of the particular fund you are looking for.

How many of their investments they disclose will depend on the fund. If you can't find the details on their website, try a web search for the exact name of the fund in full, as sometimes business websites will give summaries of their investments. You could also try calling them up and asking if there is a list you could see. If you are looking at a fund for particular employees – for example a local government employees' pension fund – you could ask the employees to ask for you, if you can get in touch with them. Contacting their union might be a good place to start.

FOLLOWING THE CHAIN...

As companies can themselves be owned by other companies, you may need to look through the ownership details of a chain of companies before you get to the ultimate owners of the company (see section 2.3). This information may be in the company's accounts (see page 54) so check them first.

But things get difficult if people are investing through 'shell' companies to deliberately hide their identity. Companies or individuals invest through another company they own, so that the name of the company shows up on the official documents instead of their names. The shell companies they

CASE STUDY: Divestment campaigns

Palestinians and Palestine solidarity activists have worked to identify the shareholders of the companies profiting from illegal Israeli settlements, in order to put pressure on them to withdraw their investments.

They have sifted through company publications, annual returns and corporate news sources and databases to put together an increasingly comprehensive list, to track exactly where the profits made from Israeli's occupation of Palestine go.

Because of this pressure, several investors have sold millions of pounds worth of shares in companies such as Caterpillar, which makes the bulldozers used to knock down people's homes. At the time of writing, Dutch pension fund PGGM has just divested tens of millions of Euros from five Israeli banks in response to public pressure.

are investing through often only exist 'on paper' and are mostly registered in countries or states with minimal disclosure requirements, meaning you can't see their annual return or the documents you need to find out who owns them.

People can also use trusts to hide their identity (see page 26). For trusts, it may only be the name of the trustee – often a lawyer – that shows up in the trust's names and details.

Nominee companies – mostly formed by a bank or another investment manager to hold and administer shares or other assets on behalf of the owner – can also play a similar role.

There is often no way round this. According to the Economist magazine: "the trail has gone cold in many a criminal probe because law enforcers were unable to pierce a shell's corporate veil". But try searching for the exact name of one of these companies on the web or in the business databases listed in section 3.5. It's a long shot, but you could also ask the company they are investing in to see if they'll tell you. Again, corporate databases can often help to find details of their 'beneficial' ownership (i.e. who is eventually receiving the money that is going through them). At the time of writing the government is considering forcing UK-registered companies to disclose their beneficial owners for public scrutiny, though time will tell how much more transparent things actually become.

RETURNS TO OWNERS

Find out how much the owners of a company are receiving in dividends from the accounts (see page 52). To find out how much they have received in total dividends, you'll need to add up the figures from the accounts of each year they owned the company.

You can find how much owners of **private limited companies** bought and then sold a company for from the accounts from the relevant years, usually in the directors' report at the front. It is more difficult for **publicly-listed companies**, but if you know when investors bought and sold shares, you can cross-reference this with the share prices on the relevant days from the London Stock Exchange's website.

DIRECTORS

If you can't find details of the directors on a company's website or in its annual report, its annual return lists a company's secretary and directors (see page 65 for more on the anual return). Companies update details of changes of directors with Companies House as and when they occur. Since October 2009 directors have not been required to give their home address, and so most just give their company's. However, if the director has been serving since before then, and hasn't changed address, you can just go to a previous annual return to find their address. You can also try searching the **Electoral Register** or a people-finder website like **123people** or **People Tracer**. The latter two also have details of any **county court cases** they have been involved in. To find out if a director has any history of **bankruptcy**, contact the Insolvency Service, part of the Department for Business, Innovation and Skills, or use the free search function on their website. More and more company directors and senior staff are now on **social media** sites like Linkedin, which sometimes include contact details and a bit more background.

You can search Companies House for details of **disqualified directors**. If you have a subscription with the premium Companies House Direct service (which charges a monthly subscription fee), you can also search by current and former directors, to see any other directorships they currently hold or have previously held – very useful for mapping corporate links. Some of the free online databases listed in section 3.5 allow you to search for directors, and much of the information contained in the annual report and other Companies House documents.

DIRECTORS' PAY

The annual accounts will usually contain some details of directors' pay – at least how much the highest paid director is getting (see page 52). The 'related party transactions' note, towards the back of most accounts, will detail any other financial transactions between directors and the company (see page 54). The annual reports of bigger companies – and especially those that publicly-list their shares – will often provide a more comprehensive breakdown of their directors' 'remuneration', including salary, bonuses and pension contributions. They will often give details of their directors' employment history, including political and civil service positions held.

COMPANIES HOUSE

Every UK company is required to file its accounts, annual return, and any change of name, director, address and other details, every year at Companies House, the state registry body. These documents are publicly available from the Companies House offices in Cardiff or London, or from the Companies

House website. Either way, you'll have to pay £1 for each document. The website holds accounts since 1995 from all current and dissolved companies. For information prior to that, you'll have to phone up and make a special request. Companies House will send you a copy of all the archived documents they have on DVD. This costs £20 per company and takes a few working days to turn around.

When you're searching Companies House, make sure you've got the name of the company exactly right. If it's part of a group, there may be other companies with very similar names. If in doubt, check the company number, which doesn't change when a company changes its name. Remember that Companies House is only a registry body. It doesn't check the documents filed to see if they have been completed correctly or if they are accurate. This can allow companies to get away with not publishing all the information they are supposed to and may mean you see some mistakes in the accounts. If you say "according to figures filed at Companies House" before quoting figures then it's not your fault if they're wrong (as long as you quote them accurately!).

Every country has it's own equivalent of Companies House. A web search for something like 'company register' and the name of the country should bring up the one you're looking for.

Several free online databases are springing up that present summaries of company accounts and annual returns (see page 74) but it's worth getting the originals from Companies House to check the figures are correct.

CAMPAIGNS, COMMUNITY GROUPS AND UNIONS

There are far too many UK-based campaigns, community groups and unions to list here so below are a few pointers for where to look to get the contacts you need. For groups outside the UK you could try media sources in the country or region you're looking at, or ask a UK group that's working on a similar issue to see if they have any links.

CAMPAIGNS

Some of the most practical, useful and in-depth research on what companies are up to is produced by the people resisting them, who will often dig far deeper into a company's operations than journalists and researchers – and over a longer period of time.

The False Economy and EarthFirst websites currently have lists of anti-austerity and environmental campaigns respectively.

The Housmans World Peace Database contains contact details for more than 3,000 national and international peace and related organisations.

The Indymedia website contains information from and about campaigns and groups across the UK.

The Mines and Communities website contains information on anti-mining campaigns and the social movements involved in them.

The Corporate Watch website has a links page with details of anti-corporate campaigns.

Check the sources in the non-corporate research and mainstream media sections below for more leads.

COMMUNITY AND VOLUNTARY GROUPS

Even if they're not involved in campaigns or resistance against the company you're looking at, local community and voluntary groups can be good places to meet people who have been affected by its operations.

Local councils have lists of community and voluntary groups in their area (although they might not advertise details of groups they see as too radical).

Most areas will also have a Voluntary Action association and these will have information on local groups. You can get details of your nearest association from the National Association for Voluntary and Community Action.

TRADE UNIONS

As well as putting you in contact with a company's workers, trade unions produce research and briefings into companies, industries and the privatisation of public services.

Wikipedia has a good list of UK trade unions, with links to their websites. Check the LabourStart and Labournet websites for union news and contact details. The Libcom website has details of workers' struggles in the UK and around the world.

NON-CORPORATE MEDIA, RESEARCH AND INFORMATION

The not-for-profit organisations, media outlets and websites below all publish research and journalism about companies from a critical perspective. This is by no means a comprehensive list, and is very UK and US - and English language - focused. They are all UK-based unless otherwise specified.

BANKWATCH
Central and Eastern European network for monitoring the activities of international financial institutions.

BUREAU OF INVESTIGATIVE JOURNALISM
Based at City University London, pursues journalism "of public benefit".

CARBON TRADE WATCH
Research collective looking at climate change and environmental issues.

CENTRE FOR CORPORATE POLICY (US)
Works to curb corporate abuses and make corporations publicly accountable.

CENTRE FOR RESEARCH ON MULTINATIONAL CORPORATIONS
Netherlands-based group. Works on issues related to sustainable development.

CORNER HOUSE
Research group producing work supporting democratic and community movements.

CORPORATE CRIME REPORTER
US-based newspaper and website exposing corporate crime.

CORPORATE EUROPE OBSERVATORY
Belgian group. works to expose and challenge influence of corporations and lobby groups in EU policy making.

CORPORATE RESEARCH PROJECT
US-based. Assists community, environmental and labour organisations in researching companies.

CORPORATE WATCH
Of course!

CORPWATCH
US research group (unrelated to Corporate Watch).

COUNTERCORP
US organisation, raises awareness of how corporations operate.

CRITICAL INFORMATION COLLECTIVE
Website collects publications by the collective, social movements and NGOs.

CROCODYL
Collaborative research website containing company profiles and reports into corporate abuse.

COUNTER CURRENTS
Indian website running articles on economic globalisation and resistance.

DEMOCRACY NOW!
US daily news show, available online.

DOWN TO EARTH
Indian magazine and website on environment and science issues.

ECO STORM
Investigative agency on green, human rights and animal welfare issues.

ETHICAL CONSUMER
Magazine and website contains lots of critical articles on a range of companies.

MORNING STAR
Daily left wing newspaper and website.

NEW INTERNATIONALIST
Magazine and website that reports on issues of world poverty and inequality.

OPEN DEMOCRACY
"Digital commons" of news, analysis and opinion from a wide range of contributors.

PLATFORM
Arts, activism and research group focusing on the social, economic and environmental impacts of the global oil industry.

POWERBASE
Website documenting corporate PR, spin and propaganda activities, with profiles on lots of companies.

RED PEPPER
Bi-monthly magazine and website of left politics and culture.

REEL NEWS
Activist video collective who publicise and share information on grassroots struggles via a bi-monthly newsreel.

ROAR MAGAZINE
Online journal providing perspectives from "the global struggle for real democracy".

SCHNEWS
Weekly direct action newsheet published in Brighton.

SOURCEWATCH
US website publishing original reporting and investigations into companies.

SPINWATCH
Publishes articles and investigations into the public relations industry.

TRANSNATIONAL INSTITUTE
Dutch group, carries out radical informed analysis on global issues

WIKILEAKS
Publishes often huge batches of information from state and corporate whistleblowers. Many other websites are emerging to publish leaked or hacked information, so keep an eye out for those too.

Z COMMUNICATIONS
US website and magazine of radical journalism and analysis.

MAINSTREAM MEDIA

All the major UK news broadcasters, newspapers and news websites report extensively on companies, sometimes critically, sometimes not.

Be aware of the politics and biases of the source. The biggest newspapers are themselves owned by big corporations, subject to the whims of their proprietors and unlikely to offend too much the companies they depend on for advertising revenue.

Find the sources used in an article or report if you can and cross-check them before using them yourself. Contact the journalist concerned directly to ask about their sources, or for information that didn't make it into the story. You can search for all the articles a journalist has published on the **journalisted** website.

BUSINESS SECTIONS

In addition to coverage in their main news output, all major media groups have specialised business sections. As a rule of thumb, the general news output of a broadcaster or paper will be a better source for critical details of a company's operations, while the business section will be better for details of investment, ownership and corporate finance. The editorial line may not be the same as for general news output, and is usually more unquestioningly pro-corporate.

LOCAL MEDIA

Regional media groups have much less funding than they used to but may still contain lots of useful information about what companies are up to in a particular area. They are also more likely to cover campaigns against particular companies, especially around things like privatisation of local services or factory closures.

INTERNATIONAL NEWSPAPERS

Use the onlinenewspapers website to find newspapers from around the world.

ARCHIVES

The British Library has one of the world's largest collections of newspapers, which includes more than 750 million pages of local, regional and national newspapers, along with periodicals covering every aspect of life in the UK and beyond. You can search their collection on their website or by going down to the library itself (see page 11). Many local, university and business libraries also have CD-ROMs of various media sources.

As of 2014, the British Newspaper Archive, a partnership between the British Library and brightsolid online publishing, is digitising up to 40 million newspaper pages from the library's collection. It's free to search but you have to pay to access material.

PRIVATE EYE & WHICH?

Special mention for the not-exactly mainstream Private Eye, which always has lots of original and in-depth investigative journalism digging into companies. Which? frequently runs investigations into companies from a consumer perspective.

BUSINESS-TO-BUSINESS

Providing news, analysis and information on companies and the market is itself a very profitable market. If you are following a particular company or industry, you can get lots of useful information from business sources that you won't find in usual news sources, such as details of a company's ownership and financing, its business model and plans for the future.

Don't forget though that their target audience is business people who are more interested in a company's revenue and profitability than the social and environmental effects of its operations (unless, of course, they affect its profitability!).

When we use these sources at Corporate Watch, we're usually more interested in the facts they contain, rather than their analysis or estimations.

Some of it may be useful – with analyses of companies' financial positions often revealing what a company's PR would prefer to ignore – but don't assume all that you read from these organisations is correct.

The generally positive analysis of banks published by the majority of corporate analysts just before the financial crisis is just one example of the lack of objectivity often provided by corporate analysis sources.

Remember that corporate websites store information about you by using cookies (see the web search section). Sites which offer free registration or free trial subscriptions are harvesting email and postal addresses to use in future marketing.

SPECIALIST BUSINESS MEDIA

As well as news and market updates, most of the outlets below will provide company profiles, financial information such as turnover and profit, number of employees, names of directors, areas of business, share price and so on.

The Financial Times remains the best way to keep up with developments in the corporate world, its preoccupations and peccadilloes. You can only read a limited amount of content for free online.

Other useful business newspapers, broadcasters and websites include Reuters, Bloomberg, CNBC, Wall Street Journal, Business Week, International Business Times, Forbes and the MorningStar and efinancialnews websites.

DIRECTORIES

Bigger public libraries will usually have the print versions of at least one or two of the directories below. Most are now accessible online but are very expensive. Many directories start with a guide to using them – reading this guide can save a lot of time.

And don't forget the **Yellow Pages** and the **Phone Book** still do the trick for most office contact details.

WHO OWNS WHOM

Tells you how more than 7.5 million companies worldwide are legally structured and shows their corporate family trees. The various volumes give details of a parent company and its subsidiaries.

D&B BUSINESS REGISTERS
List all UK businesses with five employees or more, or turnover of more than £250,000, alphabetically by county and town. Also include details of head office and branch information, names of directors, partners or proprietors, turnover, profit and loss, number of employees, net worth and company registration number. Entries are further cross-referenced by industry.

KOMPASS
Provides business information to be used by companies for sales, marketing, research and purchasing. Covers over 60 countries worldwide.

For each site listed for a company, it gives broad ranges within which turnover, profit, number of employees fall. Sometimes this refers to the whole company and sometimes just to that specific site. Also tells you the precise(ish) products and services the company supplies.

PENSION FUNDS AND THEIR ADVISERS
Provides financial and contact information for the UK's major pension funds and details of their advisory firms.

WHO'S WHO
Contains autobiographical information on more than 33,000 currently "influential" people. Not a business information source as such but contains lots of CEOs and business people.

Note the entries are autobiographical: the information is requested from and provided by those included so it's not going to be the most critical. Some public library logins will get you into the online version. **Who's Who in the City** does the same as Who's Who but for the city and also contains personal contact details. **Who Was Who** goes back to 1897 and includes entries on 90,000 people included in previous editions of Who's Who.

CRAWFORD'S DIRECTORY
Includes links between major companies, their management and their professional advisers.

IoD BUSINESS DIRECTORY
Maintained by the Institute of Directors, a business trade association and lobby group. Allows you to search businesses across the UK by name or type of business. Free access online, but registration is required.

ONLINE DATABASES
The **DueDil** and **Company Check** websites both contain freely accessible summaries of millions of company accounts and other details registered with Companies House.

DueDil has a corporate structure mapping feature that can be very useful for visualising a company's subsidiaries, parents and the overall corporate group it is part of.

The **opencorporates** site also lists companies from around the world including their filings with Companies House and equivalent registry bodies.

The **London Stock Exchange** website has brief profiles on the companies listed on it and provides latest market news and updates, with lots of information on share trading, both present and historical. It shows significant changes in share holdings, which can be used to identify major shareholders in a company.

The rest of the databases below are very expensive to access, but they contain information that it is hard to get anywhere else. Some have details of publicly-listed company shareholders that you can't get through Companies House or free business websites, for example.

However, most offer a free trial, which often allows you to access a decent amount of content for a limited period. They'll only give these out to people they think are likely to pay for the full service though and will usually phone you to discuss what you want to use them for.

You can access some at copyright or business libraries (see page 11). If you're a student - or know one - you may be able to use Athens or other academic logins. Industry bodies like the Institute of Directors give their members access to a lot of the websites below and most corporate media groups will also subscribe to them.

ORBIS
Covers 120 million companies worldwide and includes comprehensive lists of shareholders, corporate structures and lots of other very useful information.

Bureau Van Dyke, its Belgium-based owner, also produces the Fame and Amadeus databases that specialise in companies in the UK and Ireland and Europe respectively. The Zephyr database describes itself as "the most comprehensive database of deal information". Updated hourly, it contains information on mergers and acquisitions, stock market listings, private equity and venture capital deals and rumours.

FACTSET
Information on the ownership of publicly-listed companies worldwide. Claims to hold details of stocks held by 28,000 institutions, 41,000 funds, and more than 400,000 insiders and stakeholders from over 120 countries with daily updates and history from 1999. Also provides analysis of UK share registries.

MORNINGSTAR COMPANY INTELLIGENCE
Claims to provide detailed information on more than 500,000 private companies including in-depth biographical facts on more than 42,000 active and former directors and officers including their hobbies, interests, direct connections, and remuneration; financial data from annual reports and company announcements; the latest regulatory news; and company key dates and ratios. Contains the old Directory of Directors publication. No relation of the left-wing newspaper!

THOMSON ONE BANKER
Designed to "provide bankers, private equity and venture capital professionals, lawyers, consultants and academics with market news and quotes, plus comprehensive reference data to monitor changing market conditions and to gain important insight into a company, industry or event."

Another Thomson Reuters' site, LoanConnector, lets you track loan and bond transactions around the world. Includes the DealScan service.

LEXISNEXIS DOSSIER

Part of the Reed Elsevier corporate group, online database designed for legal, risk management, corporate, government, law enforcement, accounting, and academic markets. Claims to have information on 80 million companies, 80 million business executives and 1,000 industries.

GRAYDON

"Credit information" company that provides credit reports on more than four million UK companies through its website. Could be useful if you think the company you are looking at is having financial troubles.

IMPORT GENIUS

International shipping online database based in the US and the Virgin Islands. Can be useful for tracking the movement of goods around the world.

ONESOURCE

Now predominantly online, OneSource provides information on businesses, industry and executives to "make business professionals more effective and productive in completing their critical daily tasks".

CREDIT RATING AGENCIES

As well as dolling out their (in)famous credit grades, Moody's, Standard & Poor's and Fitch – who together control around 95% of the ratings business – provide lots of information about the companies they are rating, usually for free on their websites, with registration.

ANALYST REPORTS

Corporate analysts make their money advising investors on whether to buy or sell a company. They generally specialise in one industrial sector and have detailed knowledge of the companies within that sector and their financial performance.

However, unless you know a sympathetic insider you will have to pay a lot of money to get hold of them. Some reports are available on the web for a price, and the Dialog and Bloomberg Professional websites are worth checking out. Both offer a free trial period – or allow you to buy reports on a one-off basis. Brief free reports can be accessed at the Seeking Alpha website. Many banks, private equity, auditing and accountancy firms also publish some free reports from their in-house analysts.

MARKET RESEARCH

Market research firms gather information on markets, business sectors or the public, which is then sold to companies. They produce guides explaining the main trends and issues in a particular market sector and describe the main companies involved.

Major market research firms include Mintel, Nielsen, Ipsos MORI, Datamonitor, Euromonitor, Keynote, Market Strategies International and MarketResearch.com.

Most continue to publish printed reports or briefings and some libraries have market research publications in their business section. Some are published in journal format and then bound so you'll need to look through the index of the most recent one to find the issue that you need. Most companies publish all their work online, though the more detailed information will usually be paywalled.

INDUSTRY BODIES

Trade Associations are funded and founded by businesses from a particular sector to organise networking, representation, PR, lobbying and advertising activities. Professional institutes are usually not-for-profit bodies that represent the interests of a sector.

These organisations often have information services, which you can phone up to ask for statistics, market data or other information. However, they will generally charge you if you need more of their time than just speaking on the phone. You can also ask them for advice on how to do your research, or for pointers to good websites, directories, journals and libraries.

The following publications and websites can help you find the trade association or professional institute for the industry you're tracking:

TRADE ASSOCIATION FORUM

CONFEDERATION OF BRITISH INDUSTRY

UNITED KINGDOM PROFESSIONAL BODIES AND TRADE ASSOCIATIONS

DIRECTORY OF BRITISH ASSOCIATIONS AND ASSOCIATIONS IN IRELAND

GATEWAY TO ASSOCIATIONS (US)

International directories are inevitably less comprehensive, but try:

ENCYCLOPAEDIA OF ASSOCIATIONS

WORLD GUIDE TO TRADE ASSOCIATIONS

DIRECTORY OF EUROPEAN INDUSTRY AND TRADE ASSOCIATIONS

The Wikipedia website has a list of international professional associations.

Two paywalled corporate online databases – EBSCO Business Source Corporate Plus and Nexis – provide access to thousands of trade journals and other information sources. EBSCO offers a free trial and it is possible to access Nexis with some Athens academic accounts.

TRADE JOURNALS AND MAGAZINES

The best bit of trade journals tends to be the news section, though there may occasionally be some informative feature articles. It may be worth flicking through the last year or two's back issues. Trade journals often have an index in the first issue of the year, covering the previous year, or one is inserted when old editions are bound.

There is a huge range of trade journals and magazines, in a huge variety of industries. Ulrich's Periodicals Directory is a good place to start. First published in 1932 and founded by the chief of the periodicals division of the New York Public Library, it is kept in the reference section of some libraries and is also available online. The full directory is paywalled but a free trial period is offered.

Call the London-based Periodical Publishers' Association or the relevant trade or professional association for the industry you're interested in and ask what they recommend. The media section of the Guardian newspaper's website also has a page on trade magazines. Some of the bigger trade journals are listed below. All are in print and their websites are paywalled, unless specified otherwise:

BUILDING
Some free news on the site.

CONSTRUCTION NEWS
Introductory 'stubs' of the articles on the web and free e-mail updates. Also offers a free trial.

MINING JOURNAL
Stubs of the articles on the web and free e-mail updates.

MINING MONTHLY
Stubs of the articles on the web and free e-mail updates. Also offers a free trial.

MINING
Web only. Free to access.

THE ENGINEER
Covers a range of engineering sectors from transport to nuclear power and the arms trade. Website is free to access.

JANE'S DEFENCE
Produces defence review, plus journals on fighting ships, aircraft, mines, missiles etc. Lots of free online content and offers occasional free trials to the magazine.

PROCESS ENGINEERING
Lots of free online content and free e-newsletter.

FARMERS WEEKLY
Free news on the site and free e-newsletter.

THE GROCER
Stubs of the articles on the web and free e-mail updates. Also offers some free trials.

PUBLISHERS WEEKLY
Some free content on web and offers free trials.

CAMPAIGN WEEKLY
Information on the advertising industry. Lots of free online content.

HEALTH INVESTOR
Limited number of articles for free on the site. Free trial offered.

EDUCATION INVESTOR
Limited number of articles for free on the site. Free trial offered.

FLIGHT INTERNATIONAL
News on the civil and military aviation industries. Free articles and archive on the site.

AVIATION WEEKLY
News on the civil and military aviation industries. Stubs of articles on website. Some free trial subscriptions.

OIL AND GAS JOURNAL
Some free content on site and offers free e-newsletter.

THE BANKER
Free online access with registration.

INTELLIGENCE ONLINE
Security/intelligence industry research. Some options for 'free' subscriptions.

DIRECTOR
Published by Institute of Directors, claims to reflect the "real issues and interests" of their members. Free access to most online content.

You could also contact some of the **main publishers of trade journals** to ask them if they produce any relevant titles, or look at their websites:

REED BUSINESS INFORMATION
Provides several web-based data services and owns a variety of titles spanning several sectors including FlightGlobal, Farmers Weekly and Estates Gazette. Also organises conferences and events.

EMAP
Large range of titles covering retail, construction, healthcare, local government, architecture, jewellery and 'opportunities' for business in the Middle East. Also organises corporate events.

HAYMARKET PUBLISHING
Publishes titles on PR, marketing, the automotive industry, the army, wind power, waste and healthcare, plus web resources and on-line forums.

WILLIAM REED BUSINESS MEDIA
Publications and websites on food and drink, including hospitality, meat, grocery and alcohol industries, plus cosmetics and pharmaceuticals. Organises expos, award ceremonies and events. Runs some free listings.

THE HEMMING GROUP
Publishes magazines on transport, highways and engineering, surveyors, builders, retail and local government. Organises expos, conferences and award ceremonies on the same sectors.

INFORMA
British company which sells databases of information on various sectors including the pharmaceutical industry, healthcare, telecoms and media as well as publishing books and journals. Owns Taylor and Francism which includes the publishing imprints of Routledge. Organises a range of corporate events including the Monaco Yacht Show and the Adam Smith Conferences.

Other **corporate events organisers** include:

FT LIVE
Part of the Financial Times. Organises a conferences including on banking and finance and telecommunications.

UBM
British company organising corporate events globally

CLARION EVENTS
London-based organiser of corporate events including DSEI, one of the world's largest arms fairs. Sells lists of attendees at their events to corporate marketing executives.

GOVERNMENT AND PARLIAMENT

There's a list of all central government departments, agencies and non-departmental public bodies, and links to their websites and contact details, on the **gov.uk** website. It contain news updates, descriptions of the body's work and career details of ministers and senior civil servants – very useful for tracing corporate trails.

The Scottish, Welsh and Northern Ireland governments have their own websites detailing their departments and agencies, as do local authorities.

If the information you're looking for hasn't been made public, try making a Freedom of Information request (see section 3.10).

If you're investigating the dealings between a company and a public body, try talking to the **public sector staff**. You may be able to get useful information or leads by speaking to the employees of a hospital department angry at its planned privatisation, for example. Go down to the site and try to speak to people there, or get contacts through the trade union.

There are often contact details for the **civil servant** responsible for a particular piece of work at the bottom of government publications, so you can give them a call or send them an email to ask them about it. The worst they can do is refuse to talk to you, and you'd be surprised how much some civil servants are willing to talk about their work.

You can also ask your MP to ask a **parliamentary question** of the relevant minister.

Non-ministerial departments and other public bodies that may be especially useful for company research include:

INTELLECTUAL PROPERTY OFFICE
Responsible for granting patent and trademark rights in the United Kingdom. You can search by company, patent or trademark name. Also check the **EU Trademark Office**.

LAND REGISTRY
Records and registers the ownership of land and property in England and Wales. Keeps and maintains the Land Register, where more than 23 million titles – the evidence of ownership – are documented. Each title costs £3 to download from the website.

OFFICE OF FAIR TRADING
UK's consumer and competition authority. Holds information on credit licences granted to companies and publishes investigations into various market sectors.

COMPETITION COMMISSION
Conducts in-depth investigations into mergers and different industry areas and markets. Check the Competition Appeal Tribunal for details of cases involving competition or economic regulatory issues.

UK TRADE & INVESTMENT
Helps UK companies get work in international markets. Good source of information for deals in various industries and for details of

government's role helping companies set them up.

SERIOUS FRAUD OFFICE

Investigates and prosecutes fraud, bribery and corruption. Criticised for being too weak but provides details of cases and good for leads.

HMRC

UK's tax authority. Comes in for a lot of stick for letting multinationals off the hook but its website contains useful briefings on a range of tax and general corporate issues.

NATIONAL AUDIT OFFICE

UK public auditor. Audits central government accounts and, even if you may not agree with their conclusions, its reports are full of detail on the spending of public money in a variety of sectors.

OFFICE FOR NATIONAL STATISTICS

Responsible for collecting and publishing statistics related to the economy, population and society at national, regional and local levels

NATIONAL ARCHIVES

The official archive of the UK government, based in Kew, Surrey. Entrance is free and you don't need to book. You can look through telegrams, minutes of meetings, policy documents and a host of other records going back 1,000 years. You can search for records related to a particular company. Only around five per cent of The National Archives' records have so far been digitised, but this is increasing.

REGULATIONS AND LEGISLATION

You can find the full texts of all past and present UK legislation on the **legislation.gov.uk** website, part of the National Archives. Check the websites of solicitors' firms or legal associations for explanatory briefings or articles to help understand particular pieces of legislation.

To find legal cases involving a particular company, use the **British and Irish Legal Information Institute**'s website for details and judgements of UK and European court cases.

Regulators such as the Health and Safety Executive, Food Standards Agency, Financial Conduct Authority, Office of Rail Regulation, Environment Agency and Ofwat produce lots of statistics and information about the sectors and companies they are regulating.

Their websites hold the full texts of the various **regulations** that companies in a particular sector or industry have to abide by, in addition to links to the relevant pieces of UK or EU law. They also publish the full texts of the **licences** that companies are granted to do a certain type of business, allowing you to see whether companies are sticking to the **terms and conditions** of the licence, and their **duties** under them.

The exact names and responsibilities of UK regulators are often changing so contact the Department of Business, Information and Skills for a comprehensive and up-to-date list, or check the Focus on Enforcement part of its website. The Wikipedia website also has a long list.

PARLIAMENT

Use **Hansard** – the official report of parliamentary proceedings – to find out what's going on in the House of Commons and the House of Lords. Reports of the latest proceedings are published on the **parliament.uk** website and updated during the day.

The text of Daily Debates in the Commons and Lords are published online the following morning by 6am and is available in hard copy. You can find lots of detail here, with many parliamentary questions leading to new disclosures by the government of its relationship with companies, so it's well worth taking a bit of time to search around.

Registers of Members' Financial Interests let you keep tabs on which parliamentarians are making money on the side from corporate 'engagements'. Both houses of parliament publish and update their registers regularly and these are available in print or from the parliament.uk website. Councils and other public authorities publish similar documents.

The **Electoral Commission** is the elections watchdog and regulator of party and election finance. Their website holds easily accessible details of donations and loans made to all political parties, and their statements of accounts. **Companies' accounts** also have details of this (see page 55).

Parliamentary Select Committees produce reports that – while you might not agree with their analysis – often include useful facts and examples. Look in the appendices to see all the evidence submitted – there are usually many details and opinions that do not make it into the main body of the report.

You can watch most committees' sessions on the parliament.uk website, which also contains transcripts (published in print through Hansard).

Run by mySociety, a project of registered charity UK Citizens Online Democracy, the **theyworkforyou** website keeps tabs on MPs and peers. It contains information on their voting records, participation in debates and committees, and their register of interests. You can also make Freedom of Information requests through the site.

Equivalent information about your local council and councillors is available from their websites or by contacting the council office.

CASE STUDY: As the coalition government's Health Bill passed through parliament, Social Investigations combed through the registers of Members' Interests and found over 200 MPs and peers had recent past or present financial links to companies or individuals involved in healthcare.

Many of these companies have gone on to win contracts made possible by the legislation and healthcare campaigners have used the research to show the influence private companies have over the 'reforms' process.

PUBLIC PROCUREMENT AND PRIVATISATION

Central government, local councils and other public bodies together pay more than £220bn a year to companies for a variety of goods and services, including office stationary and furniture supply, computer upgrades, road building, weapons supply, management consultancy, and the provision of public services such as healthcare, education or welfare provision.

The legal framework for government procurement and details of other regulations can be found through the **Cabinet Office**. Details of the procurement policies of councils or other public bodies can usually be found on their websites, or by contacting them directly.

The **Treasury** website contains a range of details of government spending across departments, including spreadsheets bringing together details of Private Finance Initiative projects, for example.

Many public sector organisations keep lists of **approved suppliers** for certain types of work, particularly low-value contracts. If you can't find it on their website, contact the government department, council or other public body concerned to find out if they keep one and how you can have a look at it.

All contracts with public bodies are subject to the **Freedom of Information Act** so information provided by the suppliers in their tenders must be disclosed to anyone who asks for it, unless it's exempt (for example, if it's a trade secret) or would cost too much to retrieve. Companies can also request a non-disclosure agreement if any of the information in their tender is commercially confidential (see section 3.10 for more details and how to make an FOI request).

When you get a contract, you may find it's been heavily 'redacted', and key details of, for example, the revenue the company can make from it has been blacked out. If you can't successfully challenge this using FOI rules, try the **accounts** of the company and the public body to get the information you're looking for.

Companies' accounts often break down their sources of revenue, allowing you to ascertain how much they are making from the public sector. You can often find how much hospital trusts are paying for Private Finance Initiative contracts by looking in the liabilities and finance costs sections of their accounts, for example (see section 2.6).

Other sources containing details of **public sector contracts** include:

CONTRACTS FINDER

At the time of writing, the government's new Contracts Finder website includes contracts worth £10,000 and above from UK central government departments and public bodies, such as libraries, museums, and regulatory and advisory bodies. Many local authorities place their notices on Contracts Finder, and more plan to do so in future.

Contracts Finder lists contracts that have been signed since October 2010, plus contracts that are currently being tendered and those 'in the pipeline', giving you a chance to challenge them before they have been signed. You can also find out which companies currently have contracts with the government and what services they are providing.

It's free but you have to register for certain services.

For contracts that have already been awarded, Contracts Finder will usually contain details of who it was awarded to, its value, how the supplier was selected, whether the supplier will subcontract any of the work and a copy of the contract itself.

If you can't find anything on Contracts Finder, contact the relevant public body or check their website to find out what they are buying.

Scotland, Wales and Northern Ireland have their own public sector procurement websites:

☐ Sell2Wales
☐ Public Contracts Scotland
☐ eSourcing NI

SUPPLY2HEALTH

The Supply2Health website has details of the contracts that NHS bodies are giving out to outsource and privatise their services. The NHS Supply Chain website has details of NHS procurement for general goods and services.

GOVERNMENT PROCUREMENT SERVICE

Executive agency of the Cabinet Office created by the coalition government to "save money for the public sector by improving supplier management". Also responsible for agreeing centralised contracts for government departments.

OFFICIAL JOURNAL OF THE EUROPEAN UNION (OJEU)

Official gazette of record for the European Union. Public sector buyers have to place an advertisement in the OJEU if a new contract is worth more than a certain amount. This is currently just over £113,000 for supplies and services with central government.

TENDERS ELECTRONIC DAILY (TED)

Online version of the OJEU. All of the UK contracts on TED are automatically listed on Contracts Finder so you might not need it for UK research, but it's useful for other EU countries.

GOVERNMENT OPPORTUNITIES

Industry trade journal for companies interested in "government procurement opportunities" in the UK and globally.

PPP FORUM

Industry body for UK infrastructure public–private partnerships.

INTERNATIONAL PROJECT FINANCE ASSOCIATION

Not-for-profit association dedicated to promoting and representing the interests of private companies and public sector organisations in project finance and public–private partnerships throughout the world

PROJECT FINANCE INTERNATIONAL

International trade journal run by

ThomsonReuters. Published every two weeks in print, and updated daily online. Free online trial available.

SMALL BUSINESS RESEARCH INITIATIVE (SBRI),

Provides funding for new projects that "connect" the public sector with "innovative ideas from industry".

ENTERPRISE EUROPE NETWORK

EU body that says it "helps small business to make the most of the European marketplace". Information held on the site includes contact details of more than 600 "business support" organisations, many of which are UK-based.

CONSTRUCTIONLINE

Public-private partnership between Capita and the Department for Business Innovation & Skills publishing details of construction contracts offered by public bodies. Costs from £90 per year to register though.

CRITICAL SOURCES

For critical research and analysis of privatisation projects across the UK, Europe and globally, see the **Public Services International Research Unit**, based at the University of Greenwich, and the **European Services Strategy Unit**, based in Kerry. Both produce in-depth, analytical reports on the effects of privatisation on public services.

The Centre for Public Services, which has now become the ESSU, published an **Investigator's Handbook** in 2003, for looking into companies, organisations, government and individuals.

INTERNATIONAL INSTITUTIONS

Companies get a lot of work from the **World Bank** and its affiliates such as the **International Finance Corporation**, the **Multilateral Investment and Guarantee Agency** and the **International Centre for Settlement of Investment Disputes**, both through direct procurement and their notoriously pro-business policies.

Their websites and printed publications also have a great deal of information on what companies are up to around the world. Don't get bogged down in their analysis and prescriptions however – their default 'solution' for 'developing' countries remains to bring in more companies and corporate investment.

The London-based NGO the **Bretton Woods Project** keeps a critical eye on the activities of the World Bank and the International Monetary Fund.

Other international institutions include:

REGIONAL MULTILATERAL DEVELOPMENT BANKS

The websites of institutions such as the **African Development Bank, Asian Development Bank, European Bank for Reconstruction and Development** and the **Inter-American Development Bank** have similar regional information, with the same caveats.

WORLD TRADE ORGANISATION (WTO)

Records the various international trade agreements it brokers, as it follows its mission to make the world as corporate-friendly as possible.

UN BODIES

Of United Nations bodies, those particularly relevant for anyone doing corporate research are the **United Nations Conference on Trade and Development** (UNCTAD), the **International Labour Organisation** (ILO) and the **United Nations Development Programme** (UNDP).

EU BODIES

The **European Union** and **European Investment Bank** websites produce lots of research, facts and statistics about companies active in Europe. Again, any analysis on these sites should be read very critically.

The websites of many of the organisations above also contain databases of statistics that may be useful for research. If you're looking into the scale of corporate power for example, you may want to compare a country's GDP to a company's revenue.

If you're researching a mining company, you may want to find out about a country's mineral exports, or if you're investigating banks, you may be interested in data relating to the size of the financial sector as a proportion of a country's economy, or the amount of state aid they receive.

FREEDOM OF INFORMATION

A Freedom of Information (FOI) request can uncover information that those in power would rather was kept secret.

Although the regulations do not, for the most part, extend to the private sector, being able to get hold of contracts between government departments and companies, statistics, performance data, emails or details of meetings between ministers and company representatives can reveal behind-the-scenes lobbying, revolving doors between the public and private sectors, compromised planning or policy-making processes and the performance of companies running public services.

What follows is only intended to be an introduction. **The Campaign for Freedom of Information** has produced a comprehensive and easy-to-use guide, available to download from their website. There is lots of information on the **Access Info Europe** human rights organisation's website, and **Your Right to Know**, a book by the journalist Heather Brooke, last published in 2006, remains a very useful resource. **The Information Commissioner's Office** also produces their own guide to using the FOI regulations.

THE LEGISLATION

The **Freedom of Information Act**, passed in 2000 and fully implemented in 2005, established a 'right to know' legal process through which anyone can make a request to a public authority or government department. That authority must then disclose the information or provide valid reasons under the Act for refusal.

The earliest such provision was passed in Sweden in 1766 and today ninety-five countries have passed some form of Freedom of Information legislation.

If the information required relates to the environment or to an authority providing a public service it will be covered by the **Environmental Information Regulations** (EIRs), which also came into force in 2005. The EIRs are a product of a European Union directive and tend to grant a stronger right of access than the FOI acts.

The FOI Act applies to all UK government departments, Parliament, the Welsh and Northern Ireland assemblies, and all public authorities in England, Wales and Northern Ireland. This includes local councils, NHS bodies (hospitals, trusts, doctors' surgeries etc), police, armed forces, regulators, quangos, the BBC, advisory committees, museums and publicly-owned companies. It does not cover courts and tribunals, or the security and intelligence services. There is a full list of public bodies on the gov.uk website.

The EIRs also cover private companies providing environmental services, consulting or research for public bodies. **The Freedom of Information Act (Scotland) 2002** applies to the Scottish Executive, Scottish public authorities and the Scottish Parliament, and, while broadly similar to the UK act, it offers some increased access to information.

The Acts are enforced by the UK Information Commissioner and the Scottish Information Commissioner.

WHAT INFORMATION CAN I ASK FOR?

The Act covers any recorded information held by a public body, regardless of who created it or when. This can include paper records, emails, information stored on a computer, videos, maps, photographs, audio recordings and handwritten notes. Information which is known to officials but not recorded is not covered.

You can also ask for information which may not be contained in one document. This means you can ask specific questions about a topic, or for information to be extracted from a database, rather than relying on the documents that the authority already holds.

The Act requires every public sector organisation to have a **publication scheme** that describes the types of information it publishes, or intends to publish, along with any charges it applies. These schemes should be available on the authority's website and you can also request a hard copy. They must have been approved by the Information Commissioner and are legally binding. If an authority refuses to publish information specified in its publication scheme you can ask the Information Commissioner to take enforcement action.

Before writing a request, check what documents the authority has already published in case what you are looking for has already been made available. Usually, the best place to look is the authority's website. You can also contact the member of staff responsible for FOI. Disclosures from all government departments are currently listed on the **gov.uk** website. The **whatdotheyknow** website allows you to browse all requests made through the site, and the responses.

MAKING AN FOI REQUEST

An FOI request must be made in writing, either by email, a letter or a fax. You must provide your name and an address where you can be contacted (which can be that of the organisation you are writing on behalf or, usually, an email address). A request made anonymously or under an obvious pseudonym is likely to be treated as invalid. You don't have to be in the UK or a UK citizen to make a request. You can also specify how you want to receive the information: for example, in 'hard copy' (printed), by email or on disk.

The structure is simple. Just write something like:

> **TO WHOM IT MAY CONCERN**:
>
> I am writing under the Freedom of Information Act to request...

then describe what you want, ending with your name and address.

Saying that you are applying under the FOI Act is a good idea, not because the request would be invalid without it, but because it reminds the authority to follow the correct procedure when dealing with the request. If your request is for both environmental and non-environmental information, cite both the FOI and the EIR acts. Some people also like to remind the authority of its various duties under the regulations.

The Act is 'applicant blind' which means that the identity or motive of the individual requester should not be taken into account when deciding whether to disclose information (unless the request is deemed to be 'vexatious'). There is therefore no need to state your reasons for your request: the test is whether the information can be made public, not whether it can be disclosed to you as an individual.

Other key points to remember when drafting a request include:

☐ Don't include any personal opinions, complaints or anger in your request.
☐ Don't bombard them with questions.
☐ Design your request to sidestep exemptions in advance (see below).
☐ Keep your request separate from any other correspondence with the authority.
☐ Keep copies and a detailed log of all correspondence related to your request.

The request will be valid as long as it is sent to the correct authority – it is not your responsibility to find the correct individual but it's sensible to **send it to the authority's FOI officer**, if they have one.

You can also send the request to the person who deals with the issue in question if you know who that is, or to the relevant minister, chief executive or press officer (if you are a journalist). Some authorities will have an online request form, though remember to make your own copy of the request if you use this. It's also possible to make a request via the whatdotheyknow website, in which case the request and the results will be published online.

If you're not sure about your request you can ask the authority you are writing to for advice. They are obliged by law to provide reasonable advice and assistance to anyone wishing to make a request for information. This can include help ascertaining what information is recorded by the authority or what they have already published, as well as assistance in framing the request in the most effective way and advising if there are likely to be any exemption problems. The authority should also provide assistance if you have a disability that means you are unable to write a request.

Authorities should **not take any longer than 20 working days** to provide the information you asked for, or explain their reasons for withholding it. Under the UK FOI Act, authorities are permitted to extend the normal 20 working day period by another 20 working days if the request is especially complicated or long. Some may cite lack of staff time as a reason for a delay. Requests under the Scottish FOI Act and EIRs must be dealt with within 20 and 40 working days respectively, with no other permitted extensions.

Sometimes, authorities will try to drag the process out, making extension after extension. If this drags on for months, it may be time to consult the Information Commissioner, or at least threaten to.

GETTING REJECTED

If your request is denied, you have the right to be told why. If disclosure was deemed to be against the 'public interest' then the reasons should be given.

In most circumstances you should be told whether the authority holds the information you are requesting. However, if the request would not have been disclosed in any circumstances – for example if it related to court records or the security services – then the authority is unlikely to reveal whether or not it holds the requested information.

COST LIMIT

Among the most common ways for a body to reject a request is by claiming it would cost too much to find and deliver the information, so you need to make yours as specific and unambiguous as possible. Requests to the Ministry of Defence for "everything you hold related to BAE Systems" are easily rejected, for example.

For a government department, the cost limit is £600, equivalent to three and a half days work at a fixed rate of £25 per hour. For all other public authorities the limit is £450. Authorities may only use the costs of locating, retrieving, extracting the information, putting it into any special form that you requested and redacting (obscuring) any exempt information. They may not include the time taken to decide whether or not they have to disclose the information.

If you know the documents you want, for example minutes of a particular meeting, a specific report or a set of figures, then describe them as precisely as you can. Alternatively, you can make a request for a particular type of record produced over a specific time period, such as correspondence or emails between the authority and another party over a given period.

For example, a request for all correspondence between the Department for Work and Pensions and Atos Healthcare is probably going to get rejected. A request for all correspondence between the Minister of State for Disabled People and Atos Healthcare between January and June 2013 stands more of a chance.

You can ask for more than one thing, as long as it doesn't exceed the cost limit. You could, for example, also ask for minutes of any meetings that occurred between the minister and Atos for the specified time period.

If you send in lots of separate requests on the same subject, the authority may aggregate them into one request if they are made within 60–working days of each other, and then use the cost-limit to refuse the request.

Requests may also be aggregated if, in addition to being made within 60 working days of each other, they are made 'in concert' (i.e. if the requester's name is different but the authority believe the requests originate from the same individual or organisation).

Under the Scottish FOI Act, the authority must answer each request separately.

If you're told you're exceeding the

cost limit just make another request for less information. You can also ask the authority's advice on how to narrow your request to within the cost-limit so that you receive at least some of the information you requested.

Cost limits work differently under the EIRs, under which the authority may issue you with a 'reasonable' charge for information that exceeds the cost limits (which are set at the same level as under the FOI act).

EXEMPTIONS

The FOI regulations are also riddled with exemptions that authorities can cite as reasons for not disclosing information. However, they are not always deployed correctly and require careful scrutiny to ensure you are not being denied information you are entitled to.

The authority must show why the information is exempt, and that the public interest in not disclosing is greater than the public interest in doing so. Do not simply accept the authority's use of an exemption without checking the legislation yourself first.

It is worth remembering that if the public interest in disclosure and the public interest in withholding are judged to be equal, then the authority must disclose the information. Similarly, if there is little public interest in either withholding or disclosing the information, then the authority must disclose it.

The list of exemptions to which the Public Interest test applies to is long. For a full list see the legislation on the Ministry of Justice's website.

COMMERCIAL INTERESTS AND CONFIDENTIALITY

The most relevant exemption for getting information about companies is probably section 43 of the act, which sets out an exemption from the right to know if:

"the information requested is a trade secret, or release of the information is likely to prejudice the commercial interests of any person." (A person may be an individual, a company, the public authority itself or any other legal entity.)

The Information Commissioner's guidance expands on this, saying "a commercial interest relates to a person's ability to participate competitively in a commercial activity, i.e. the purchase and sale of goods or services. The underlying motive for these transactions is likely to be profit".

This is a frequently cited reason to deny information relating to companies but the exemption is still subject to the public interest test so it can be worth appealing – explaining why the public interest in disclosure outweighs any 'harm' caused.

To make things more difficult, the commercial interests exemption very often overlaps with section 41, which sets out an exemption from the right to know where the information requested was provided to the public authority in confidence. Companies are fond of **commercial confidentiality** clauses when signing contracts and these can be hard to get around.

In deciding whether the disclosure of a particular piece of information would be harmful or beneficial to the public, a great deal of judgement is exercised by

CASE STUDY: SERCO AND PATHOLOGY

In 2012, Corporate Watch made the below FOI request to Guy's and St Thomas' hospital trust, to find out if GSTS Pathology, the joint venture between the trust and outsourcing company Serco was quite as successful as the company was claiming.

The trust disclosed minutes of the hospital's monthly evaluation meetings and performance results that showed the company repeatedly missing targets and a series of worrying clinical incidents, including one patient receiving "inappropriate blood due to patient history not being flagged" and kidney damage results being calculated incorrectly after a software fault. A similar request to Bedford Hospital – where GSTS had also won the contract – showed many staff were increasingly discontented, with one consultant complaining there had been an "unacceptable" increase in the number of errors and incidents since GSTS took over.

To whom it may concern

I am writing under the Freedom of Information Act to request:

Copies of all reviews – including yearly, half yearly and interim reviews – of the performance and progress of GSTS pathology services at Guy's and St Thomas hospital trust in 2011 and 2012

Regards

XXXX

public authorities' information officers. The dominance of market ideology and a culture of secrecy mean that the emphasis is often on protecting short-term commercial interests at the expense of transparency and accountability.

The important thing to bear in mind if you receive a refusal claiming commercial confidentiality is that the authority must be able to prove that the information being refused would really must have a prejudicial effect on of the company involved if disclosed. The test must rest on the content of the document in question, not its type (tenders, contracts etc).

Another important point to recall is that the commercial interests exemption does not necessarily compel the authority to refuse the whole document, but rather to redact the sensitive information in it so you can't see it. A public authority may disclose a contract with a company, but redact details of financial returns, for example. The right to know under EIRs is stronger for this and many other exemptions. For instance, they do not allow for commercial confidentiality to trump the public right to access information about emissions.

PUBLIC POLICY

Other exemptions that may be of particular interest to anyone looking into the relationship between companies and governments are those that cover the formulation of public policy. They are phrased to include everything relating to the process, not just advice. It is very rarely adjudicated in the public interest to disclose information prior to the decision being taken, so you might be better off making your request after the policy has been formulated. The two main concepts hindering disclosure are:

1. 'Safe space' i.e. preserving an environment in which policy-makers can make decisions without being distracted by criticism or public pressure.
2. 'Chilling effect' i.e. ensuring that policy-makers are able to conduct and record their policy-making free from fear of future disclosure of its details.

These two factors will diminish over time, especially if there has been a change of government in that time.

More positively, following a request by Friends of the Earth, the Information Tribunal adjudicated that there is no expectation of privacy for senior government officials or lobbyists meeting each other or their attributed comments, declaring:

"there is a strong public interest in understanding how lobbyists, particularly those given privileged access, are attempting to influence government so that other supporting or counterbalancing views can be put to government to help ... make best policy".

Decisions made on exemptions are all collected online and the Information Commissioner's Office has detailed guidance on all the exemptions.

APPEALING

A negative reply should also inform you of what to do to appeal the decision and how long you have to do so. You will usually first appeal to the authority itself, requesting an internal review.

Explain as clearly as you can why you think the authority was wrong to reject your request and cite any supporting legislation, previous cases and decisions made by the Information Commissioner. The onus in not on you to prove the authority's wrongdoing, but for the authority to prove that it has complied with the law.

You can also request a review if you are not happy with how your original request was handled or if you think the authority does hold information it claimed not to in the original reply (minutes of meetings whose existence were denied have miraculously been found after an internal review, for example). If the authority again rejects the request, you can **appeal to the** **Information Commissioner.** Again, be as clear and specific as you can about why you think the authority is wrong, making the public interest case for disclosure, and including copies of your request, the initial appeal and any other correspondence and emails with the authority. Remember to check the Commissioner's website for specific advice on making requests.

If the Commissioner upholds your request they will issue the authority with a notice requiring it to disclose the information to you, or to do whatever else is deemed necessary to comply. If the authority disobeys this notice they can be held to be in contempt of court and in theory, may face a fine or even imprisonment. If you're not satisfied with the Commissioner's decision, you can **appeal to the Information Tribunal** (as can the authority). The tribunal can then be **challenged in the High Court** but only on a point of law. Controversially, both UK and Scottish ministers have a veto which allows them to overrule certain decisions made by the Information Commissioner. The use of this veto must not be secret and may be judicially reviewed.

CASE STUDY: An FOI request by Corporate Watch about asylum accommodation provided by private landlords in 2008 was refused by the UK Border Agency, which argued that releasing the information requested "would be likely to prejudice the commercial interests of both the UKBA and those companies with whom the UKBA enters into contracts," as this "could give rise to a potential risk to the UKBA's ability to negotiate contracts in the future, and therefore inhibit the Agency's ability to achieve value for money."

After an appeal, the Information Commissioner overturned the original decision, agreeing that "there is a significant public interest in knowing details about the value and length of contacts awarded by government departments, especially those which are for such a large sum of money."

Therefore, the public interest in accessing the information requested "outweighs that in withholding it and should have been released to you in response to your original request."

FUTURE CHANGES TO THE FOI ACT

Governments tend not to be too fond of FOI regulations. New Labour seemed to regret passing the FOI Act very soon after they'd passed it – Tony Blair wrote in his memoirs that he "quakes at the imbecility" of it.

At the time of writing, the Coalition Government is seeking to restrict the right to information provided by the FOI Act by making it easier for authorities to

CASE STUDY: MILITARY LICENSES

It can sometimes take a long time to get the information you're looking for. The Campaign Against the Arms Trade (CAAT) spent a year and a half trying to get information out of the Department for Business, Innovation and Skills (BIS) about which companies had applied for licences to export military equipment, and what the destination countries were.

They started by asking for the names of companies that had applied for licences to repressive regimes like Bahrain and Saudi Arabia, requesting information on some of the most controversial weapons categories which included tear gas and sniper rifles. They eventually got BIS to disclose all companies that had applied for arms licences to any country in 2010 – i.e. just before the brutal suppression of many of the popular uprisings in the Middle East and North Africa. This information was enough to allow anti-arms trade groups to go to companies based in their local areas with solid proof that they had intended to sell military equipment to a particular country, and put pressure on them to stop doing so. The request below has paved the way for further requests for information for other years, and has allowed CAAT to better piece together the details of the UK companies profiting from wars and repression around the world.

Dear BIS

I would like to request a list of the names of all companies that applied for licences for the export of equipment with Military List ratings during 2010. I would like the companies to be listed by destination country.

I anticipate that the simplest format for the list would be a spreadsheet with just two columns – one for company name and one for destination country.

Yours

xxxx , CAAT

refuse requests on cost grounds. all who use the FOI Act and limit its reach.

The Campaign for Freedom of Information are campaigning against these changes. Contact them for more details.

INDEX
for descriptions of corporate and financial terms
(Note this is not a full index for the handbook. To find other information use the contents and quick links pages at the front.)

GET IN TOUCH

Corporate Watch runs workshops and training days on how to investigate companies and on specific topics such as company accounts or the Private Finance Initiative.

Call 02074260005 or email contact@corporatewatch.org if you'd like to request one for a group you're involved in, or keep an eye on our website for details of any upcoming ones.

And please get in touch if you have any suggestions regarding this handbook, or if there is anything you'd like to see added, or changed, for the next edition.

SUPPORT OUR WORK

Corporate Watch is run on a tight budget and we need your support! We do our best to avoid dodgy funding, we don't take money directly from companies or governments, and we provide all our work for free online. If you like our work, please consider helping us with whatever you can afford. Even small amounts will help us stay independent and sustainable.

Make a one-off donation or become a 'Friend of Corporate Watch' for £5 a month (or more if you like). Not only will you be providing us with regular funds, but you will receive paper copies (or digital if you prefer) of all our publications as they come out.

Get in touch at 02074260005 or contact@corporatewatch.org, or see our website for more details.